PRACTICAL ISSUES IN EMPLOYMENT TESTING

D1295856

PRACTICAL ISSUES IN EMPLOYMENT TESTING

Robert G. Rose, Ph.D.

PAR Psychological Assessment Resources, Inc.
P.O. Box 998/Odessa, Florida 33556

Library of Congress Cataloging-in-Publication Data
Rose, Robert G.
    Practical issues in employment testing/Robert G. Rose.
      p.   cm.
    Includes bibliographical references.
    ISBN 0-911907-09-2
    1. Employment tests—United States. 2. Employment tests—Law and legislation—
United States.   I. Title
HF5549.5.E5R668   1993
658.3'1125—dc20

                                                                        93.27798
                                                                           CIP

PAR **Psychological Assessment Resources, Inc.**
P.O. Box 998/Odessa, Florida 33556/Toll-Free 1-800-331-TEST

9 8 7 6 5 4   Reorder #RO-2465   Printed in the U.S.A.

Acknowledgments

My gracious thanks to my editor, Serje Seminoff, who was extremely helpful and supportive at every step. His thorough knowledge of practical testing issues made him the ideal editor. The book was reviewed by Dr. Joan P. Brannick, whose excellent comments were extremely helpful in patching up some holes in the initial text. Attorney Edward Mitchell of Thompson, Hine and Flory, Cincinnati, Ohio, was immensely helpful in explaining legal aspects of testing and in commenting on the manuscript. Thanks to Dr. Kal Lifson who first taught me to translate psychological jargon to meaningful business language. My assistant, Jayne Davila, wrote and proofed the manuscript and, as usual, kept me from making silly mistakes. Dr. Pat Rose, of course, is my constant counsel in all things. If there are any heavens, Jo Rose will surely have one of blood-red roses. Good suggestions and comments in this book were probably paraphrased from someone else, as all mistakes are mine alone.

Preface

This book has a very specific purpose. Let's talk about what it is and is not designed to do.

It is not intended to replace standard textbooks dealing with testing. It does not, for example, give formulae for calculating a correlation nor does it cover the history of testing. On the other hand, it can be a good adjunct to the standard text: read this book first and you'll understand the more in-depth text more easily.

There are only a few citations in the text itself. If you are interested in any of the relevant sources of information, you can go to the chapter notes at the end of the book, but that isn't necessary to understand this text. If you want general sources of information, these are also listed in the appendix.

This book is intended to give a solid overview of the field of employment testing. If you are involved directly with testing, you must have the basic information covered in these chapters.

If you are indirectly involved with testing, you can use the tests at the end of the book to select psychologists, human resource directors, and attorneys. None of the self-test information is speculative or arguable—it's fact.

Within the last month I have encountered a psychologist doing testing who thought it was necessary to validate tests in every case, a Human Resources Director who asked if a test had been "validated by EEOC," and a lawyer who advised his clients not to use testing and to rely on the interview—apparently unaware that an interview is a test, a very vulnerable one.

These aren't just mistakes—they are unpardonable blunders that could cost you dearly. Any expert who scores less than very high on the tests has not done his/her homework.

You will learn best by reading each chapter and its relevant notes, even if some chapters are of less interest and/or simply a refresher. On the other hand, time is a scarce resource for many of us. You may want to browse through different sections, or skip some entirely. Let's look at an overview of the book chapters:

Chapter 1—What Is a Test? The term *test* is used in different ways by different sources. You can avoid some silly surprises by being sure you know what is implied by test.

Chapter 2—Statistical Issues. Statistical terminology and statistical issues pervade any discussion of testing. Don't be afraid of statistics! Yes, you could spend several years of your life getting a Ph.D. in the field. At the same time, some of the concepts basic to the application of statistics in testing can be understood in an afternoon.

Chapter 3—Validity. The issue of test validity comes up repeatedly. There are several different types of validity, and, while they are related to a central concept, the types can be quite different. You're going to hear this word used a great deal, often inappropriately. For example, if you've ever heard someone say, "this is a valid test," it means they didn't understand the concept.

Chapter 4—Test Development. The manner in which a test is developed may be very important for your use. There are several ways to develop a test, each with its strengths and weaknesses.

Chapter 5—How to Use a Test. The manner in which a test is used is the major issue of importance. Tests can be used to derive a narrative description of some personal issue to an impersonal five-digit score. And each usage can be reasonable—or unreasonable—depending on the circumstances.

Chapter 6—Common Employment Tests. There are scores of tests. By understanding some of the more common types, you can better understand the field of testing.

Chapter 7—Testing Programs—Ideal and Real. Let's think about the ideal world, that is, the textbook version you seldom see, and the real world. The real world is a long way from the ideal BUT that's no reason for slipshod test use.

Chapter 8—Legal Issues. If you use testing in an industrial setting, you must consider legal issues. Even if you are an attorney you may find that the legal issues are quite different than you imagine!

Chapter 9—The Interview and Other Alternatives to Testing. People often feel that testing is risky, but they forget to ask: what's the perfect alternative?

Chapter 10—Issues of Frequent Concern. Testing affects people, and anything that affects people will have some attendant concerns about ethicality and effectiveness. Some issues are real, others are simply the result of misunderstanding.

Chapter 11—Future of Testing. Where is it going? Where should it be going?

At the end of each chapter you will find questions. Try to answer these questions to be sure that you have really read the chapter. Finally, take self-tests at the end of the book and score yourself. Take a test now if you're confident of your testing knowledge.

If you read a term that confuses you, go to the glossary to review the definition. The Appendix gives you various sources of information if you wish to do further test research on your own.

Testing is greatly misunderstood. Intelligence tests do not measure culturally invariant characteristics of the brain, and neither are they specious and temporary representations of middle-class white values. Personality tests are not infallible X-rays of the soul but they are powerful in some of their behavioral predictions. This book will help you separate fact from nonsense, and it will help you learn where and when you can use the valuable tool of testing.

Table of Contents

CHAPTER 1

WHAT IS A TEST?

- A test is a standard device to measure skills, intellect, personality, and other characteristics.
- Everything you do in an employment setting is a TEST by legal standards.

Defining a Test

In the next two chapters, we give definitions for many terms. One term, however, is so important that it rates a chapter of its own: *test*. This term is used in many ways. When most people hear test they think of a paper-and-pencil test that yields a score. That is one definition, but in this book we will use the term test even more broadly to refer to *any standardized device that is administered in oral, paper-and-pencil, computerized, or any other medium and which yields a score, rating, description or category*. We will limit the scope of the definition by excluding medical testing.

As broad as the above-stated definition is, it is not nearly as broad as the definition used by the Equal Employment Opportunity Commission (EEOC) and the courts. Legally, everything used in personnel action is a *selection device*, and that means *everything*. Anything that can in any way impact a selection, promotion or other decision at work is a selection device.

If someone tells you about the special problems relating to testing, it is best to go directly to the Uniform Guidelines (UG)—as of 1993, still the authoritative guideline for hiring. Here is the EEOC definition of selection device: "Any measure, combination of measures, or procedure used as a basis for any employment decision. Selection procedures include the full range of assessment techniques from traditional paper and pencil tests, performance tests, training programs, or probationary periods and physical, educational, and work experience requirements through informal or casual interviews and unscored application forms" (Uniform Guidelines, §16, Q). In other words, everything!

Ah, but perhaps that's only a definition. In practice, do the courts give some special sanction to non-pencil-and-paper devices? No. As we will see in chapter 8, interviews and performance reviews have been challenged in the courts and have been found wanting. It's not just an empty definition.

In using tests in an industrial setting, especially for the purposes of hiring, you will commonly encounter the old "to test or not to test" debate, which is a meaningless debate, since there is no way to avoid testing! Managers and personnel directors must understand that they are *testing* if they do anything to hire people.

A test is a method for making a discrimination among people. In employment settings this method is often used to help in hiring decisions. No one can choose to test or not to test, because *testing is inherent in any form of selection*—the choice is one of doing the best possible job of testing.

What a Test Measures

As you will see in the following chapters, there are specific skills tests (e.g., knowledge of Civil War history), interest tests (e.g., your interest in carpentry vs. sales) personality inventories (e.g., whether you are outgoing or shy) and cognitive tests (also called intelligence tests, intellectual tests: math, vocabulary, reasoning tests, etc.)

At the simplest level, a test measures interests, intellect, personality, skills, and so forth *at the time of testing*. So what does a test result today mean about behavior tomorrow? Quite a bit.

Think of the mental aspects of a person as analogous to physical aspects. Can someone change his/her height? As a child, certainly; as an adult, very unlikely aside from the fractional increase and decrease in the waking cycle. Can someone change his/her weight? Yes. But, as weight clinics demonstrate, it's not always easy. Can someone change physical strength? Again, gyms are testimony to the fact that strength can be changed and that it takes some work!

Some things, like the length of your hair, can change instantly if you so desire. Some things, like height (at least between adulthood and advanced old age) are almost unchangeable. Some things, like weight and physical strength, are changeable but take a lot of effort. If you weigh 1,000 people today and weigh those same 1,000 next year you will find very little change, despite vows to go on diets; people can change, but they usually don't.

People can improve intelligence, to a certain extent. People can change personality, to a certain extent. People can learn to enjoy new interests. People can gain new skills.

Momentary feelings of anxiety may change rapidly. Personality traits may be modified through counseling; for example, a person who is pessimistic may become more optimistic. People can change intelligence by increasing vocabulary, studying logic, and practicing thinking. Those changes are like changing weight. People can do it if they try hard; most people won't, even if they say they will. Read the chapter notes for chapter 10 to learn about the stability of personality, intelligence, and interests.

Knowing someone's physical strength or health may be important in some situations and not others. No one can lift 7,000 lb.; practically anyone can lift a pencil. No matter how healthy you are you'll probably catch the common cold every year.

In the same way, cognitive and personality factors can't be viewed in a vacuum; they must be considered relative to the situation. You will read more about this in the chapter on validity.

STUDY QUESTION

- Do the EEOC Guidelines apply only to paper-and-pencil tests?

CHAPTER 2
STATISTICAL ISSUES

- You have to understand *some* statistics—and you can!
- Such terms as *significant* and *variance accounted for* are often misunderstood.
- Statistical concepts are simply logical ways of describing situations and making decisions.

Many of us are uncomfortable with mathematics. And that branch of mathematics known as *statistics* can be pretty bewildering. Unfortunately, to understand testing you have to understand some statistics. Don't worry! It's true you could spend 8 years getting a Ph.D. in statistics, but you can learn to understand the statistics related to testing in an overall sense very quickly. Let's start by with a story about a hypothetical test-use situation. If you can understand the story, great—you have a good overall grasp of test statistics. If you don't understand it, it will probably be a confusion over the italicized words. Read through the pertinent sections and then re-read the story.

The ABC Math Test

Jim Smith is using the ABC Math Test to select people for his management trainee group. The test is based on one of the *test scales* of a larger test. He has established a *cut score* of 16. That's the *raw score,* and it is at the 25th *percentile* of his *norm group* of previous management applicants. He figures it is reasonable to exclude the lower one fourth of applicants. He does not do *race norming*—everyone must meet the same standard.

In doing analyses, Jim was glad he had good *samples* of the trainee *population.* Jim has given the test twice to the same people and says he found that the test *correlates* with itself .70. He is glad that the *reliability* is .70. The test company has recently produced an *alternate form* of the test, and he plans to use it in the future.

More importantly, he argues that his test correlates .39 with success in the training program as measured by trainer's *ratings* on a 1–5 scale. He feels that success in the training program is a *reasonable criterion*. This *validity* correlation of .39 is *statistically significant at the .05 level*. He also used number of weeks to complete the course as a criterion, and he found an *inverse relationship, a strong negative correlation* between the score and the time taken to complete the course. He has some *descriptive* statistics from the period when the test *was being validated* and has shown that the *mean* of trainer ratings is 3.9 for people who score above the cut score and 2.5 for those who score below. An *inferential* test has shown this *difference* between the means to be *statistically significant*. In short, he feels he has a lot of *empirical evidence* that proves his test to be *criterion valid.* He will keep this test and perhaps add others in a larger *test battery*. One of Jim's advisors has argued that some of the correlations and other statistical findings are significant but not *practically meaningful*, but Jim feels that he can demonstrate good *utility.* He is continuing to do research with his tests even though there is a *restriction of range* since the tests are now being used in selection. Using his measures in classification of candidates, he finds that he gets a high percentage of *hits* and not too many *false positives*.

Jim is pleased with the results. While there is a *restriction of range*, he notes that the distribution of test scores and the *distribution* of criterion scores are *normally distributed*.

Jim realizes that some of his results could be due to chance, but he will attempt to *replicate* his findings and does not think there will be much *shrinkage* of results.

Here's What It Means

Test scales

A single test may measure several related things. For example, one part of a test may measure basic math and another may measure trigonometry. The different parts can be scored separately and are referred to as *scales*. In some cases the scales can be added together to get an overall score, for example, a cognitive test may have a verbal and quantitative score, which can be added together to give a total intelligence score. In other cases it makes no sense to add the scales, because they function like separate tests. For example, if you had a personality test it would usually make little sense to add the *sociability* scale score to the score for *cooperativeness*.

He has established a cut score of 16

This means that before someone can enter the program, they must score 16 or higher on the test.

That's the raw score

That just means that 16 is the score, for example, the person got 16 answers right on the test. Sometimes a "correction for guessing" is used in cognitive tests to get the raw score. Raw means it hasn't been converted to a percentile score. And, a percentile score is the next thing we discuss.

...it is at the 25th percentile

That means that someone who scores a 16 will score as high or higher than 25% of the other people in the norm group. Oh—but what's a norm group?

...his norm group of previous management applicants

In this case it is the scores for previous management applicants that are being used as the "normal" or norm group, which the group used as a standard. Please note: if he used high school graduates as a norm group, a score of 16 might be at the 60th percentile instead of the 25th, because more of the people—60% in this case—would score at or below 16. If he had used mathematicians as a norm group a score of 16 might be at the 5th percentile because very few people—only 5%—would score that low or lower. Always know the norm group and decide if you think it is appropriate.

In some cases scores are used in an *ipsitive* manner, meaning a comparison with one's self. For example, in some vocational tests (e.g., the Self-Directed Search, the SCII, and the Vocational Preference Inventory) a score pattern can tell you which interest is relatively strongest, second strongest, etc. for that individual. You would not know, however, from that score code, how the person compared to other individuals only his/her relative interests.

He does not do race norming

Some people argue that applicants should be compared to their specific race or group. For example, instead of having a cut score of 16 for everyone, the cut score would be based on the relevant norm group. Thus, anglos might have a cut score of 16, as high or higher than 25% of the anglo group, and Samoans might have a cut score of 18, as high or higher than 25% of the Samoan group. Since the Civil Rights Act of 1991, the use of race norming has been forbidden.

...sample of the trainee population

Every woman in the world is the total *population* of women—5 women is a *sample* of that population. Generally speaking, the larger a sample, the better it is as a representative population.

The test correlates

A *correlation* is a statistical measure that expresses how strongly one measurement, such as a test score for workers, predicts another measurement, such as widgets produced on an assembly line by those workers. If there is no relationship, the correlation is zero—the test score had no relationship to number of widgets produced. If there is a perfect relationship, the correlation (or more properly the correlation coefficient) is 1.00—the higher the score, the more widgets produced.

Here's another example: if you had a group of men and you measured their shoe sizes and their heights you would find that men with bigger shoes tended to be taller. Of course, some men with big feet would be short and some men with little feet would be tall. The correlation between these two measurements (or variables) would not be 1.0, but it might be close, say .79. In other words, there would be a difference in height between men with size 5 and size 7 feet, with the size 7 guys being taller and the size 10 guys being taller yet, and so on. If you measured shoe size and vocabulary, the correlation would be zero or very close, say .02.

If a correlation has a plus sign (or nothing) in front of it, that means the correlation is positive: as one measurement increases, the other does so as well. Sometimes a minus sign, or negative sign, is put in front of the correlation to indicate a negative correlation. This doesn't have anything to do with the *strength* of the relationship: it means the correlation is negative: as one measurement increases, the other decreases. A negative correlation is sometimes called an inverse relationship.

If you correlated height with distance from head to the *ceiling* it would be a −1.00: a perfect relationship with one number (distance to the ceiling) decreasing as the other number (height) increases. If you correlated height with distance from head to the *floor* it would be a +1.00 (or simply written as 1.00): a perfect relationship with one number (distance from the floor) increasing as the other number (height) increases. If you correlated years of age with future life expectancy you would get a high negative correlation, say −.70. This means that the older you are, the less years you have to live, roughly.

A correlation looks like a percentage—it is not. A correlation of .65 does not mean 65% of anything. A correlation of .50 does not mean a fifty-fifty probability. The *square* of the correlation indicates percentage of variance accounted for; for example, if the correlation is .40, it means .16 of the variance is accounted for. But don't get too excited about that—even that is not as straightforward as it looks. Read the chapter notes if you want to understand the concept of variance accounted for. The main thing to remember: don't make the mistake of thinking of the correlation as a percentage or any form of probability.

He is glad that the reliability is .70

If you correlate a test with itself, this measure is called reliability. It is a measure of the extent to which a test consistently measures the same thing. Bill and Mary take the ABC Math test today and score very high while Jim and Jack take the test and score very low. If they take the same test next week, what would you think if Bill scored low, Mary scored in the middle, and Jim and Jack, who scored so low, now score high? You would probably say the test was not very reliable.

Sometimes there are two test forms, two slightly different but higher similar versions of the same test, and they are correlated for a reliability measure. Sometimes one half of the test is correlated with the other, and this measure of internal consistency is sometimes used as a reliability measure. Reliability is affected by test length, that is, the longer the test, the more reliable it will be. In practical terms, however, it takes a great change in test length to materially affect reliability.

..recently produced an alternate form

As we just mentioned. The company has made another version of the ABC Math Test with some slightly different but very similar items, for example, item number 25 may be 50 · 5 = on form A and 40 · 3 = on form B. Forms A and B are alternate forms, different, but similar enough to be used almost interchangeably.

...ratings on a 1–5 scale

This just means that someone rated the students' performance on a scale where 1 means very poor and 5 means very good. Rating scales are often used in measuring human behavior.

A reasonable criterion

The *criterion* is a measure of success on the job, for example, widgets produced, ratings by supervisors. Just any old criterion won't do, however. What use is there in supporting the use of a test with a poor measure? A criterion must be reasonable; it must make good sense.

This validity correlation

The correlation between the test and the criterion is one measure of validity. The higher the correlation, the better the test predicts the criterion. The higher the correlation, the more valid the test.

Validity is related to reliability in a statistical sense, that is, the validity is limited by the reliability. For example, if the reliability is .64, validity cannot be higher than .80, the square root of .64 (although it could be lower). In practical terms, however, even moderate reliability can yield acceptable validity.

...is statistically significant

This concept is extremely important. It may seem elusive at first, but keep reading and it will dawn on you. It involves whether a result is likely to be due to chance.

Let's start by talking about probability. Take a dice roll. You say you can roll a seven, and you do so on the first roll. It's not likely you could do that because there are 36 combinations of the dice and only 6 of them produce a seven. The probability of rolling seven is 6 divided by 36 or .17. The dice could be fair, that is, you got that result purely by chance. The probability of rolling two sevens in a row is .028—not likely, but it could certainly happen. Again, it *could* be purely due to chance. If you roll eight sevens in a row, that should happen about once in every million six hundred thousand cases *if* the dice were fair and the result was purely due to chance. You would probably reject the idea that the dice are fair and conclude they are fixed in some way!

Just as you could, just by chance, roll a seven two times in a row, you could, just by chance, get a high correlation between two measures. Let's say you had 4 men: 2 men with little feet and small vocabularies and 2 big-footed guys with big vocabularies. Does that mean foot size is really related to vocabulary? Probably not, it's just a coincidence based on a small sample. If you got a group of 400 guys, you could still get such a coincidental result—but it's much less likely. The larger the group and the larger the difference, the less likely it is that something is due to chance.

Now we're ready for a definition: when we say that something is *statistically significant,* that means the results *could* be due to chance—there is nothing fixed about the dice, there is really no relationship between the measures—but it is unlikely. You reject the idea that the dice were fair and assume they were fixed; you reject the idea that there is no relationship and assume there is a relationship. There's one more thing to understand about significance, and that's the significance *level,* the next thing we look at. One very important note: Statistically significant difference means the groups are probably different. A lack of statistical significance does *not,* however, mean the groups are equal!

...at the .05 level

I'm not going to cry "cheat" if the dice come up seven the first time you roll, even though the probability is only 1 in 6 that it would happen. But if it happens eight times in a row where the chance is 1 in 1.7 million, I surely will think something's fishy. But where's the cutoff? At what *point* do I decide that the odds are too unlikely—1 in 10, 1 in 100, 1 in a 1,000?

The scientific community has arbitrarily established .05 as the highest probability of a chance result before we reject the idea of chance. The .05 level means that the probability of getting a correlation that *size* with that *number* of cases is less than .05, or 5 in a hundred, if the results are solely due to chance. You can also have .01, .001, and so forth, but .05 is generally the minimal acceptable level.

It's like a game with some rules we all agreed on. If the Music Test correlates with the grade in music class .33, and if that is not significant, it means the result could have been due to chance—there was really no relationship between test and grade. If the correlation is .60, and if that is significant at the .05 level, that means the probability of getting that correlation is 5 in 100 or less—and that's small enough. I reject the idea that it was a coincidence and conclude there *is* a relationship between the two measures.

...*inverse relationship, a strong negative correlation*

The higher the score, the less time it took the student to complete the course. So as score goes up, class time goes down, giving a strong negative correlation (as we discussed earlier).

...*some descriptive statistics and has shown a mean*

A descriptive statistic is one that describes some aspect of a group of scores. The mean, for example, is the average of the scores. The mode is the most frequently occurring score. The median is the score that is in the middle, higher than 50% and lower than 50%. Other measures describe the variability of scores, etc.

...*was being validated*

In the ideal situation, a test is administered and data are gathered before it is actually put into use. In this case, therefore, he had training scores of people who scored lower than the cut score, because the cut score was not being enforced during the validation research stage.

An inferential test

A descriptive statistic is like the mean. An *inferential* test relates the statistic to the significance level. You infer something about the scores. A correlation can be descriptive (it tells you about the degree of relationship). If the correlation is checked against a table that takes into account the number of cases and relates it to a *significance* level, it is being used as an inferential test.

...*difference...statistically significant*

If you have a range of scores, you will probably do a correlation showing that the higher the score, the higher the criterion measure. If instead of a range of scores you have two categories, pass or fail, you may do a statistical test to show that the two categories are different in terms of criterion scores.

In this example, the researcher showed that trainer rating (the criterion) was higher for those who passed than for those who failed. The scores were different, and the difference was significant. As you remember, this means he used a mathematical process to show that a result like his would have occurred only 5% of the time, or less, if there was no real difference in the groups. Correlations and tests of differences are just different types of statistical tests that are aimed at doing the same thing: showing that one measure (such as a test) predicts another measure (such as training scores).

...*empirical evidence...criterion valid*

Empirical means based on observation rather than theory. Criterion valid means that the validity is based on a relationship between a test and a solid success measurement.

...*in a larger test battery*

A group of tests that are administered together is referred to as a test battery.

...significant but not practically meaningful

If it is not likely that a difference is due to chance, it is statistically significant—but that may not mean it has any real *value*. Suppose I showed you statistics that people who take my diet pill for 2 months lose one tenth of a pound more than people who don't. I prove it true to your satisfaction. So what? The difference is real—it's not just chance or coincidence—but it's not big enough to make a practical difference. Who cares about one tenth of a pound?

...he can demonstrate good utility

Utility refers to the practical effect on business. Regardless of the size of the score difference, if using the test saves me $10,000 per position per year, it has good utility. Utility is a way of showing that test use is practically meaningful as well as statistically significant. In practice, even small, consistent relationships may lead to good utility. See chapter notes for "Variance accounted for."

...restriction of range

Once the company starts not hiring people who scored below 16 it's hard to say how those people would have performed—they aren't there! You can only look at the effect of scores 16 or higher, you have restricted the range of test scores. And, to the extent that the test really works, you have restricted the range of training scores. Any number of things can lead to a restriction of range, and the use of a good selection system is one of them. It's a Catch-22...if the selection system is really working, it will be hard to prove.

..."hits" and "false positives"

A hit is a person who proved to be successful (as defined by some criterion) who had passed the test. It's as though you hit the target. A false positive is a person who was not successful, but also passed the test. A lot of hits doesn't mean much if you also have a lot of false positives! If you increase hits by being more lenient, you'll increase false positives.

...distribution...normally distributed

A distribution of scores refers to the frequency, or how often, each score occurs. It's a simple way of looking at groups of scores. Here's how it works.

If you measured the weight of a group of college freshmen, you would find a few lightweight men, a few more who were slightly below average in weight, a few who were somewhat heavy, and a small group who were very overweight scores. The majority would be right in the midrange of weight.

If you plotted frequency of occurrence on the *Y*-axis and weight on the *X*-axis, you would have a bell-shaped distribution. Distributions like these are often close to a mathematical distribution called the normal distribution.

Some distributions are multimodal, meaning that they have more than one clump of scores in the middle. Some are skewed, meaning that there are an unusual number of high or low scores in the distribution.

Distributions can have an effect on statistics, but if you get into that area, you will probably need to call in a statistician. Just be aware of what a "normal distribution" refers to.

...replicate...shrinkage

Good research means you attempt to redo your research to hopefully replicate or get the same results. Shrinkage means that a strong relationship proves to be weaker when the study is replicated. This is especially likely when you use a lot of measures combined in a complex form of correlation known as *multiple regression.*

Now, go back and read that story and you'll find that it makes much more sense. If some of it still confuses you, mark those passages and try again.

If you are interested in learning more about statistics, you can find the sources in the Appendix "Doing research."

STUDY QUESTIONS

- What does reliability refer to?
- Does statistical significance (e.g., .05) refer to the percentage of time you will make incorrect decisions using a test?
- Does a correlation (e.g., .30) refer to the percentage of cases in which measure 1 will correctly classify measure 2?
- If the reliability of a test is .64, the validity can be no higher than .80, correct?
- If the reliability of a test is .64, the validity could be .20, correct?
- If a score of 19 is higher than 85% of the scores in that norm group, it is said to be at the 85th percentile, correct?
- If I have scores for 10 college women: 42,45,46,50,50,50, 51,51,52,60, what is the mode?

CHAPTER 3

VALIDITY

- Most important—validity refers to how well a test measures what it is supposed to measure.
- There are several approaches to validation, including content, construct, and criterion.
- We now realize that all validity is construct validity. All validity depends on a sound logical chain of reasoning.

First, and most basic: *validity refers to how well a test measures what it is supposed to measure.* In any discussion of validity, make sure you keep that essential core concept in mind no matter how far afield you roam in "legalese" or statistical models. There are two basic corollaries:

1. A test is only valid with respect *to something*. The claim that the XYZ Test is "valid" means nothing unless there is a specification of what it is valid for. The XYZ Test may validly measure math ability but not be valid for assessing engineering potential.

2. "Validity" is *variable*. The XYZ Math Test may measure math ability very well. It may measure ability to succeed in engineering school to some extent. It may measure far less the ability to learn mechanical drawing. It may not measure at all the ability to succeed in English classes.

The Different Types of Validity

Validation refers to support for a test being valid. There are three main types of validity, or perhaps more appropriately, three main approaches to validation: content, construct, and criterion related. Content validity is perhaps the easiest to grasp.

Content Validity

A test is said to be *content valid* if the test content is the same as the job. For example, testing someone's ability to drive a truck by having her drive a truck through a series of road tests might be said to be content valid. Choosing a baseball player by having her pick up a bat and see how many pitches she can hit would be a content valid test.

The term *face validity* refers to the extent to which a test looks valid to the person taking it. For example, a person who takes a work interest test and encounters a question about a preference for carpentry over music may find that item reasonable; a question about preference for types of food, on the other hand, might make little sense, that is, have little face validity.

While face validity may often seem similar to content validity, they are, in fact, different. Face validity refers to how the test appears to the test taker and content validity to the adequacy with which a test samples the job domain. I might find a test that asked about looking for clues to be very face valid as a test for admission to the police department. A veteran policeman might know that looking for clues was a naive idea concerning police work. The item would have good face validity but no real content.

Anyone who argues that a test is content valid must be sure that the content of the test and the content of critical aspects of the job are really similar. A test of differential equations might have no validity for a job involving change making: even though both test and job involve "math" the content of the job is obviously different than the content of the test.

Criterion-Related Validity

Criterion-related validity is purely empirical and is demonstrated mathematically. Suppose you want to select people for a computer operation. Someone has told you that music ability is related to ability to program. You decide to put that to a test.

Surprisingly, you find that a music ability test predicts success in computer programming! In fact, it works better than any other test you try. Students who score high in musical ability learn new programming languages quickly. Students who score moderate do less well, and those who score low do a very poor job. Your proof of validity is not based on the content of the test, and you have no logical reason for assuming that music ability is related to computer ability. But it is an empirical fact.

Construct Validity

If content validity is the most obvious, construct validity may be the most esoteric. Construct validity is based on a logical, theoretical argument. An example will help illustrate.

Suppose you are selecting people for a new management program. You decide to give all applicants an IQ test. In this IQ test, people must form designs with the blocks, take vocabulary tests, answer general knowledge questions, and so forth. You are challenged and must explain what form of validity you are claiming.

Is the test content valid? Well, not really. No one has to put together block puzzles or do vocabulary tests in management. The general knowledge questions certainly have no more to do with running business than with driving a truck.

Is the test criterion valid? No. You have done no studies showing a relationship between this test and management. In fact, you know of no studies that have been done for managers and this test.

You still remain convinced and you argue as follows: "This test purports to measure a trait called intelligence, the capacity to learn, to process information and reason. This test has tasks that seem logically related to those sorts of abilities. In addition, it has been correlated with other tests that purport to measure intelligence. It also correlates with such things as years of education. In the military we find that officers score higher on this test than enlisted men. In schools, A students score higher on the IQ test than C students. In short, I have no direct proof, but everything points to this test as a measure of intelligence. It seems logical that making business decisions, (e.g., being able to absorb a great deal of information and use it in a logical fashion), must be related to intelligence."

Researchers demonstrate a subset of construct validity called *convergent* validity when they show that their test is related to other similar measures (e.g., an intelligence test that correlates with other intelligence tests) and *discriminant* validity to show that the test is not related to other measures (e.g., an intelligence test that does not correlate with personality measures). This takes a lot longer to demonstrate than content or criterion, doesn't it? In addition, it is a theoretical, logical argument, and someone else may simply choose to disagree with your argument.

Building a Team

A quick analogy. You're going to build a soccer team. You want to test potential players to see if they are good enough to be on the team. You could test them by having them kick the ball and run—since that's what they actually *do* during the game, you claim your test is *content* valid.

You could test them by measuring lower body strength—no one actually has to squat with 100 lb. on her/his back during the game, but you claim that, logically, lower body strength is associated with game performance. Your test is *construct* valid.

Finally, if a friend convinces you that hours of television watched per week is a good predictor of success, you would claim criterion validity—you don't understand *why* it works, it just works.

What's the Best Form of Validity?

There are three forms of validity and people have, in the past, ranked them in order of relative strength and desirability. In order to understand current thinking, we need to approach the subject in three different passes.

Construct validity appears to be the most problematic. In fact, the Uniform Guidelines qualify the use of construct validity so much that at one time some researchers felt it was an impossible strategy. Because the argument is theoretical, there are many links between the test and the use of the test.

Content validity appears very straightforward, but in fact, it's not that simple. Suppose you are hiring secretarial candidates, and you give a typing test. Seems logical, but wait! Is typing the main thing that secretary will be doing? What about filing, answering the phone, scheduling, organizing work, etc.—is it fair to select based on a test of typing when that may be the least crucial part of the job? You stick to your guns. In this particular position, the job will involve 60% typing, and it is a crucial component. But wait! The *test* involves looking at a page and typing as many words from the page as possible in 5 minutes. On the *job*, your secretary will be typing for hours. Perhaps the test is biased toward people who "spurt work" but can't maintain concentration and accuracy.

On further consideration you realize that, in real life, the secretary doesn't type from one page to another. Rather, he/she must take some scribbled notes or a garbled dictaphone message that may say "...for the next paragraph, find that letter to Smith and say the same thing." In short, the secretary has to organize a lot of information and make some decisions. Typing speed, per se, has no great importance.

Also remember that many jobs are not characterized by what is done *most* of the time, but by job duties in extreme situations. In a validation test study for a fire department years ago, we quickly realized that firemen spent most of their days selling garbage sacks (a side business sanctioned by the city as a way of providing small additional revenue). The typical fireman spent only a small fraction of his/her time climbing ladders, lifting heavy hoses, and applying technical knowledge to extinguish fires—but those were the duties that represented the critical content of the job.

A manager may spend most of her time having casual conversations with her people—and that common activity may be critical because it keeps communication channels open. She may spend only 1 hour a month making major financial decisions—and that may be equally critical because of the importance of that decision.

Think of your football team: your place kicker spends 5% of his time kicking the ball and 95% sitting on the bench—which is the critical content: sitting or kicking?

Criterion-related validity appears to be the king of the validities and, in fact, many researchers felt it had preferred status. After all, this type of validity is empirical, that is, it has demonstrated power. It does not seem to depend on a theoretical argument. We don't have to worry about the sampling of the content because it isn't necessary—the test works, period. In addition, this is the only form of validity that is quantitative, the only form that allows you to say how valid a test is in absolute rather than comparative terms. You can say that a content-valid test or construct-valid test is better supported than alternative methods; with construct validity you have correlations and probabilities to give quantitative descriptions. In an ideal world, criterion validity is obviously best.

Now, let's talk about the real world. Let's pick on criterion validity because by so doing we will understand the other forms of validity much better.

Why Criterion Validity Isn't Best

Criterion validity seems so obviously right, so obviously scientific that it's not surprising that the 1978 Guidelines favor it. The criterion-valid model is so alluring and seems so scientific and so unchallengeable that we're going to have to take it apart. Otherwise, you may be deluded into thinking an easy answer is at hand.

You see, criterion validity would be the way to go if you had an ideal world. If you had a *criterion* that was absolutely a perfect measure of performance, or even one that was very good. If you had a *large sample size*, say 400 subjects of both genders and various races in the same job. If you hired these 400 people blindly, a random sample of the job force, and gave them all a test (any test). If you then measured the performance of these 400 people after, say, a year. If you then found that these people showed variation from high to low on this perfect criterion. And if there was a significant and meaningful correlation between the test (any test) and the criterion. Then, indeed, you could argue that your test was criterion valid. If you are ever challenged in court you simply point to your study, and since it is criterion valid, it is defensible.

Now let's look at why you are unlikely to have that ideal world.

Small samples

It is difficult to get large samples of people, even in large organizations. Remember that the Fortune 500 companies do not begin to account for all the companies nor do they employ most of the people in the United States. Ninety-one percent of businesses employ less than 20 people, just as an example. Even organizations with a 1,000 people—and that's BIG for an American company—may only have 10 people in a given job! That's not big enough to do anything, statistically. A real difference might not show up with a sample of 30 people; a difference that did show up could be due to an inappropriate sample. With samples of less than 100— and that's a big sample—some scholars argue that expert judgment is a better alternative to criterion validity.

Restricted range

This problem is an insidious one, and it's based on the simple fact that people don't apply for jobs blindly and employers don't hire blindly.

Hardwork Law School requires a score of 1,000 on the Law Test, a well-known test whose scores range from 0 to 1,800, average 900. Hardwork has a reputation for being tough. After all, look at the scores they require. Students with scores of 1,000, minimum acceptable, often apply for less-prestigious schools. So the range of scores for Hardwork is 1,000 to 1,800, and the distribution is very *skewed*, that is, the scores are most lumped toward the high side. There are more scores of 1,500 than there are of 1,100. There are 100 students and they are ranked from 1 to 100. Student 1 is great, but 100 is no slouch! And you would be hard pressed to find much material difference between 35 and 67. You do a correlation and find that there's no relationship between the Law Test and the final ranking.

So Hardwork drops the Law Test. Now, students apply who would have scored 400, and some get in. Quality drops, so now the difference between 1 and 100 is a real difference. If you tested people now, the correlation would be very strong. There was *always* a relationship, but the restriction of range masked it. It was useful as a quality control measure, but the relationship was hidden.

Concurrent versus predictive study

In the ideal world, the company was willing to let you test a lot of people who were being hired and not use the test until the validation study was done a year or so into the future. That's a *predictive* validation study: you have shown that your test predicts.

Most companies, however, already have people in place. The Mosttowns Police Department has 100 uniform officers and they hire only about 20 a year. They are required to have a test within 8 months. So you do a *concurrent* validation study, that is, you test the officers already on board and correlate those scores with previous performance ratings. You find that those officers who perform well are those who score high on your test of situational judgment. Great!

Wait, says Dr. Expert. The officers who performed well have had the opportunity to work on more cases and that experience has *taught* them good situational judgment. You have not *proven* that your test *predicts* good performance. There is good reason to believe that concurrent validity does work (see the chapter notes for chapter 10) but you can still be challenged.

Please note that ALL forms of validity are designed to insure that a test predicts accurately; predictive validity is simply one approach to substantiating that, and, if done ideally, the strongest substantiation.

Criterion

This is the biggest problem by far. In their desire to be scientifically rigorous, someone forgot a crucial fact. Yes, let's validate this suspicious test by correlating it with an infallible criterion, but wait! What is that infallible criterion? Supervisory ratings!? Read chapter 9 about lawsuits successfully prosecuted against supervisory ratings.

What is a good criterion? Is a performance rating any less abstract or subjective than a test theory? The measurement of performance is as abstract as any theory for jobs in management, for example. How do you know who's a good manager? Is it popularity with staff or work output, and how do you measure that? What makes a good policeman? Is a high number of arrests a good sign or a bad sign?

Ah, but at least for some jobs here's the answer—the naive researcher will proudly pull out financial performance data and/or widgets produced. That's concrete! Or is it...

Think about it. You have a ranking of salespeople by volume of sales. Joe Blow sold $120,000 last year, but he's an old hand who should be producing $200,000 at least. And Mary Doe only sold $30,000, but that was in her first year, and the company thinks she's great. Well, you can control for time, right? You have John Smith and Frank Earnest, both on board for 1.8 years, so no excuses. Smith had volume of $230,000, and Earnest had a measly $90,000. So Smith is better, right? Wrong! Ah yes, smiles the boss, we put Earnest in the toughest region and he's already producing. And Smith, he frowns, Smith is "cherrypicking" the easy accounts and not working on the tough customers that are likely to be long-term investments. Once you look at it, even concrete data start becoming awfully subjective.

A problem no one discusses

You have a job that demands physical strength. You find that a test of sports interests, of all things, correlates significantly with job performance! Who knows why, but it works, right?

Men are more likely than women to have an interest in sports, and men are more likely to be physically strong. Your test is biased against women and people who don't like sports. It is unfair. Sure, most men are stronger than most women. But Harvey, who loves sports, is a wimp. Mary Sue, who loves Gothic novels and hates sports, can press Harvey with one hand. Few people talk about it, but criterion validity can mask unnecessary discrimination.

Mixed messages

You may think that these are theoretical arguments. If the Uniform Guidelines favor criterion validity, why not just do a criterion validity study of some sort and be done with it.

Won't work. While the Guidelines favor criterion validity, they also point out concerns in the same areas listed above. If you do a validity study with 30 people based on a criterion of supervisory ratings, you may find that your validation is not a validation at all.

In addition, the Guidelines are just that—guidelines. Courts are not bound to make judgments solely based on the guidelines and, in fact, do not. Professionals have an obligation to use good judgment, and current psychological opinion differs markedly from the Guidelines. As one major example, psychologists today view validity not as exclusive types of validity but as different approaches to validation. In addition, they view ALL validity as a subset of Construct validity, which brings us to our next, and startling, development.

Why All Validity is Construct Validity!

All validity is construct validity! How can that be?

Think about it. Since God has not ordained a perfect criterion you can't rely simply on statistics, even if you had the large samples required. You must prove your criterion is a good one. You can't claim content validity unless you can show that your test content is a reasonable sample of crucial job duties; and how do you know what is critical?

The answer is this: you have to use a *logical chain of reasoning,* and that is what is meant by construct validity. You must have a rationale about what you are doing and why. The physical sciences have long known that you can't claim to make an observation without a theory. Logicians have long known that empirical observations (induction) lead to premises, which must then be linked logically (deductively) to reach conclusions. Psychological testing is slowly beginning to realize that you must have a logical basis. From that starting point you will want to examine the content of the test. You will want to look at criterion-related studies where feasible, placing an emphasis on choosing a good criterion. You may want to do studies even with very small samples as long as you don't make sweeping decisions based on chance occurrences.

You may feel that the jobs for which you are testing are similar enough that you can use *validity generalization.* For example, if you need a test for firemen in a medium-sized Southern town you may use a test that has been developed for Firemen in large northeastern cities. You feel that the jobs, while not exactly alike, are similar enough to generalize the validity of that test to your situation.

You may analyze the job of supervisor and find that the supervisor spends 20% of his/her day supervising others, 50% doing basic math, 10% writing reports, and 10% miscellaneous. You have no data on anyone anywhere who has exactly that job; but, you find a test that is valid for people doing basic math, another test that measures writing ability, and another that measures managerial skill. You use *synthetic validity,* synthesizing a test battery based on the demands of the job.

If you feel that your test is valid, but more valid for one group (e.g., white males) than another (black males), then you argue for the existence of *differential validity;* thus, it might be unfair to use the same test in the same way for all groups. Be aware that a great deal of evidence would be necessary to prove the existence of differential validity. In addition, there are legal problems with treating groups differently.

What approach can you take that will guarantee that no one will sue you or, if they do, that you will win? No such thing. Judges and juries are not fungible, and you can never be sure of the outcome of a trial.

Do what is best for your business and be ethical and fair. Read chapter 8 on some tips for staying out of court.

STUDY QUESTIONS

- In order to select XR9-language computer programmers, you give them a test that consists of questions relating to the XR9 language. You make no claims about underlying theory, and you have no success data relative to the test. You merely claim that the test covers the same information that programmers will actually deal with. What kind of validity is this?

- Dr. Jack Expert wants you to use the XYZ Math Test in hiring for all your hourly people. He tells you not to worry because the test is valid. Is his assertion true or false?

- Even if a test successfully predicts supervisory ratings, it may not be valid by EEOC standards and practical business standards. True or false?

- The job of secretary at Somestore Inc. involves the following important components: 20% typing, 10% filing, 10% answering the phone, 40% greeting clients, and 20% scheduling. They use a typing test to make the hiring decision. Since it is content valid, it meets EEOC requirements if it is ever challenged. True or false?

- Years of research says the job of policeman demands someone who can handle stress. I have a stress test with years of supporting evidence. But when I tested 15 policemen rated "highly effective" against 15 policemen rated "highly ineffective" good performance correlated *negatively* with stress coping, and it was significant at the .05 level! I'm not going to use the test to pick low scorers, however, because the result doesn't make sense. Good decision, true or false?

CHAPTER 4

TEST DEVELOPMENT

- Tests can be developed on the basis of a theoretical argument.
- Tests can be developed on the basis of obvious content in the test items.
- Tests can be developed on the basis of empirical relationships, even ones that are not obvious.
- Common sense and good ethics should be the overall guide in the development of any test.

You probably aren't going to be interested in developing your own test. It can be a difficult process, and many good tests are already in existence. No test is going to be exactly what you want, but a standard test will usually have enough strengths to justify using that rather than build your own. It is a good idea to know the major approaches, keeping in mind that, as with validation approaches, a combination can be used.

The Rational Approach

The rational approach is probably the easiest to understand. You develop test items based on the area you want tested. This is what any teacher or professor does when making a test for specific knowledge of course material covered in the classroom. So, one item on the "Early America" test is: "The Aztecs were a large nation in Mexico, True or False?" An item on the math test might be: "If angle ABC is 60° and angle BCA is 30°, then angle BCA is A) 90° B) 60° C) 279° D) none of the above."

The problem with the rational approach is knowing how the item will be perceived by the test taker. For example, on a knowledge test, two questions may appear equally hard to you, yet one may be easy and the other quite difficult. Two personality test items may seem related but may be actually quite different. The rational approach is often used as a starting point for developing tests or where the content of the test is very specific. The rational approach is one taken when one is interested primarily in developing good content validity.

The Factor-Analytic Approach

The factor-analytic approach is a statistical approach that involves having people take a large number of test items and then seeing which items clump together. The math is much more sophisticated than that; but that's the bottom line.

Consider the following potential test items:

"I like to deal with people."

"I enjoy starting conversations with people."

"I enjoy movies more than books."

The first two items seem obviously related to being with people; even though the third is not as obviously related, the statistical process may indicate that it is. The factor-analytic approach ensures that items in a test scale are related to each other. The shortcoming is that while the items may be related to each other in some statistical sense, they may have no practical use. So you have a group of items that clump together and measure liking for peanut butter—who cares? In addition, the approach may leave out items that are important. On a scale to measure work attitudes, the item "I never curse at coworkers" seems relatively unrelated to the other work attitudes items. You might want to leave it in because you consider that item *practically* important regardless of its statistical properties. The factor-analytic approach is a good approach to developing good *construct validity*.

The Empirical Approach

The empirical approach identifies items related to an external criterion regardless of content or internal relationship. Suppose research shows items such as "My father was a sports fan" and "Green is my favorite color" all correlate strongly with management success. You see no relationship in the content nor do you care. You don't know what "liking green" has to do with a "sports-minded father" or why either item would predict management success. You don't care because it works. An empirical approach has the same logic as criterion validity.

One problem with the empirical approach is *chance*. Remember, you can roll three sevens in a row even if it is unlikely. Since you are relying purely on statistics, perhaps the "green" item appeared only due to chance. Perhaps the response was very time and locale bound—your population came from an area where green is one of the school colors.

The Political Approach

For example, litigation recently led some test developers to start test development by selecting items that are passed equally by black and white candidates. This political approach was called "dry labing" in my college physics lab: find the desired result in the text and work backward to get it. Dry labing doesn't really do anything constructive. If the test content is not relevant to the job, it should be changed; if it is relevant to the job, tampering with it will only reduce the relevance.

Combining Items in a Score

The most common way to derive a score is to assign each item response a +1 or a 0 and add them up. For example, if you answer ten items indicating sociability, you get a raw score of 10.

A Good Approach to Test Development

In fact, none of these approaches are exclusive. It is important to start with good items. In *Soroka* a test was condemned because the items were invasive. The test proponents argue that the items contribute to an empirically valid scale, individual items being blind to the user of the test results. *Soroka* is being challenged, but regardless of how it comes out, industrial test developers are wise to avoid using weird-sounding items about urine and sex preference unless there is a *very strong* rationale. Items with good *content* do a very good job of measuring the personality traits of normal people (see the discussion of the NEO in chapter 6). Other legal cases (such as *Golden Rule* and *Allen*, discussed in the chapter notes) may also have an effect on individual items in licensing or admission tests.

Factor-analytic techniques are a good way of double-checking that items that *seem* related *really* go together. Suppose I devise a sociability scale and find that my favorite sociability item "I always like big parties" doesn't show much statistical relationship to other items on my "sociable" scale—maybe my concept of sociability being related to party going isn't accurate.

Empirical studies, especially those with solid criteria, help tie the test to practically useful measures. Once we have established that items are good and that they make conceptual sense, we want to see if they really measure anything of use.

Check the documentation of tests and find out how they were developed. Remember that there is no one right approach—and a combination of approaches is usually best.

Regardless of Which Approach You Take, Use Common Sense and Ethics as Your Guide

The American Psychological Association has standards for test development and use. On one hand, the American Psychological Association does not make law; on the other hand, this venerable institution provides us with good guidelines that are well thought out.

Tests should be documented so people can examine the manner in which they were developed and any information pertinent to their use. Tests that are not administered and interpreted by an expert should be qualified correctly as to the extent and limitation of their use. To give a 20-item, self-scored test and claim that it is an accurate picture of many intricate aspects of personality is almost certainly false. Such test could have a proper use but could be misused as well.

STUDY QUESTIONS

- A test item "I like brown dogs" is consistently related to success in mechanical drawing, even though we have no idea why—we're using this test item based on an empirical approach to test development. True or false?
- I am creating a test of judgment. I examine each item to see if it sounds like it measures good judgment based on my expert analysis of the factors involved. I am using a factor-analytic approach to test development. True or false?

CHAPTER 5

HOW TO USE A TEST

- In some cases you can rely on mathematical combinations of test results.
- In some cases there is no mathematical formula, and you have to use expert judgment.
- There are many factors involved in how to combine test scores.
- Tests can be used to develop people in addition to making hiring decisions.
- If you are going to use tests, make sure you know the distortion factors.

What do you do with test results? Some tests are straightforward and yield one easy to interpret score, for example, you scored at the 50th percentile on the ABC Math Test. In other cases, however, you have more than one score. This is often the case with, for example, a personality test, which may have different scales. You may have a score on a math test, two different personality test scores, and an interest test score. If you have more than one score, how do you use test information?

Actuarial Versus Clinical

One of the major issues you will encounter in test usage is whether tests should be interpreted in an actuarial (or sometimes termed *statistical*) versus a clinical fashion. Actuarial refers to an interpretation that is formulized and mechanical. Clinical refers to interpretation, which relies on expert judgment. Let's take an example from sports.

The Football Team

You are building a football team. Each candidate does a bench press, curl, and hundred-yard dash. Each level of weight lifted and running speed can be assigned a 1 to 5 rating. The ratings are added, and if they sum to 9 or higher the candidate passes. Your experience has shown that these candidates are more likely to be good football players. You are taking an *actuarial* approach. Once the formula is set up, no judgment is required. A clerk could do the measuring and scoring as well as a coach with 30 years of experience.

One day a player shows up whose bench press is very low and his curl only slightly better. But he can run the hundred faster than anyone in the history of the team, and running speed is something you definitely lack this year. Given this year's list of competing teams, running speed is something you can use in your offense.

You decide that his ability to run, given the needs of your team and your understanding of the sport, makes him a special case. You are relying on your judgment as an expert in football; hence, you are making a *clinical* prediction.

Which is best? The actuarial approach has the advantage of being simple. Once set up, it can be used by anyone, regardless of knowledge of the sport, whereas the clinical approach requires an expert. In addition, research shows that the actuarial approach, when based on sound data, will usually do a better job than your judgment, no matter how expert you may be. Why? Because you will forget things, make poor guesses, or let subjective factors sway you; and the formula makes none of these errors.

Is there ever a time for clinical judgment? Of course. Some situations are unique and any formula is necessarily general. In some cases you don't have enough data to develop a formula and you must use expert judgment.

An actuarial approach is best for large-scale general predictions when there is a strong experience base for the formula. A clinical approach is best when situations are unique and individual. Since most cases don't clearly fall in one category or the other, the coach may use both methods. The coach may demand certain minimum strength standards and then make individual judgments based on try-outs.

In using tests, you can interpret a test solely on the basis of a formula that weights and adds scores. That weighting and adding actuarial method is probably best if you have plenty of strong data. Based on a sound study, you may find that if you add the score of a math exam to the score of a mechanical reasoning exam you can predict which engineers will be most effective at mastering your training program.

If you have great familiarity with a test and good guidelines, you can read the scores and develop a judgment based on your understanding of the situation. You may take a test that measures introversion and another that measures interest in entrepreneurial jobs. You may decide that, based on your judgment, the sales manager needs to be very extroverted and entrepreneurial. You further decide that managers need to be entrepreneurial but not as extroverted. You don't have a guideline, but you know what the test scores mean and what your jobs demand. But remember, expert judgment is only valid to the extent that it is well-informed and well thought-out. If you don't have a definite formula to follow, this clinical method may not only be good, it may be the only method available to you!

More likely, you'll take the coach's approach and use both methods. You'll strive to do your own quantitative studies or find similar studies that will allow validity generalization (see chapter 3). Since you will probably not find such formulae for every job, you'll have to place some reliance on good judgment and even the much-maligned "gut feel."

Other Questions in Test Usage

In addition to questions about clinical versus actuarial, you have other choices in how to use scores. Do you add them or interpret them in terms of patterns? Do you rank people based on their scores and take the top 10%, or do you choose a pass/fail score and hire everyone who passes?

Configural Versus Linear

Suppose you have three test scales, A, B, and C. You do some research and find that a formula A + 3B + C predicts scale success. This is a linear formula.

Another person makes groupings according to the patterns formed by the scores. According to his/her research, if A is 5 or higher and B is 9 or higher and C is 3–9, that is one group: they are good "sales cold callers"; if A is less than 5 and B is lower than 9 and C is 10 or higher, that's another group, good at "client maintenance" and so on. He doesn't just add scores, he makes his predictions based on these different groupings of scores.

Which is best? Depends on the circumstances. Generally, the linear approach works as well or better as the more complex configural method. There are exceptions, notably the examination of the "all-average" profile. For example, assume you have a profile of say five different traits, largely independent, and this particular profile has no score in the upper or lower 25%. Most people see such a profile and assume that this is probably a very commonly occurring profile; after all, it's "just average." If you assign numbers to each scale and add them, that's right—that score is very common. If you literally mean five scores, no one of which is above or below average, *that* is a rare occurrence—only 3 in 100 people have such a profile. And that's not just a statistical oddity. In practice, people in business who are "all average" are often what organization development expert Kal Lifson (1976) terms "vanilla winners"—people who are very successful in business because they are balanced, successful because of a lack of liabilities.

Multiple Cutoff Versus Additive

Suppose you have two tests, math and reading. You feel that both math ability and reading ability are important. One approach is to set a cut score on both and demand that the person pass both. This is called *multiple cutoff*. Another approach is to add both scores and demand a minimum score on the sum. This is called an *additive* or *composite* score.

Which is best? Here's the acid test—if one score does compensate for another, the additive model works best. For example, if Jane Doe, who doesn't read very well, can still be a success *if* she does math extremely well. If John can't do math at all, but his excellent reading ability makes him very valuable. One score compensates for another. We don't want to exclude Jane just because she doesn't read; we would lose her math ability.

On the other hand, imagine someone saying, "Yes we made Bill a pilot. I know he's blind, so he scored 0 on the eye test, but he is so coordinated and so knowledgeable we felt that made up for it"; obviously it does not. That's an example of a situation where you would have to have a multiple cutoff. You have a hurdle—eyesight—which measures an *essential* trait. Any time one test or selection device is a pass/fail you must be sure it really is an essential measure.

A word of caution. In practical usage, if one test (or any other selection device) is used as a hurdle, that is, in a multiple cutoff sense, that one component becomes more important and is more likely to be challenged in the event of adverse impact (see chapter 8 on legal issues).

Raw Scores Versus Normed

To know that I scored 16 out of 20 on a math test may tell you nothing. If 90% of high-score seniors can do that, it's nothing to brag about. If only 10% of college senior math majors can do it, it's pretty impressive.

When tests are combined in an actuarial formula, raw scores are usually used. When they are being interpreted in a clinical sense, they are almost always normed. There are exceptions however. Some tests are interpreted in terms of raw scores, for example, John Holland's Self-Directed Search. We chose to use raw scores in developing a diagnostic for the computerized version of the VPI. There are some cases in which the raw score tells you more than a percentile. You have to look at the justification on a case by case basis.

Cut Scores Versus Ranking

Let's say you're choosing people for your football line and you have decided that weight counts. You can rank your candidates by weight and choose the top 10%—no specification of how heavy, just as heavy as you can get. Alternatively, you might make a cut score; if candidates are at least 250 lb, they pass that test whether 0 or 20 pass. You can do the same with test scores.

Which is best? Again, look at the circumstances. There are some situations in which a certain characteristic is vital to a certain point, but not beyond. After making the minimum weight for the heavy weight boxing category a boxer may want to become even heavier, say 225 lb versus 210 lb—but look hard and you won't find a 400-lb heavyweight boxer. While 210 lb is much better than 105 lb, 420 lb is not necessarily better than 210 lb and may be worse. In that case, having a certain cut score makes sense, ranking doesn't. In the same way, a job may require a certain level of reading ability (e.g., enough to read the labels on cans). But does that mean a person with a Ph.D. in Linguistics is the ideal stock clerk? Not likely. You only want a certain level of reading ability, say 25th percentile on the XYZ reading test. Beyond that, you don't care.

In situations where you want "the best you can get" and "the higher the better," ranking makes sense. Let's suppose I'm putting together a basketball team. Why make a "cut score" of six foot two? If the tallest 11 people range from 5 ft 10 in. to 6 ft 1 in., that's the best I can do. On the other hand, why bother with all these 6 ft 2 in. people if I am lucky enough to have a room full of people over 7 ft? Suppose I must admit 10 people to a graduate program and I have found that the Graduate Record Exam (GRE), a standardized test, is an excellent predictor of success. Why set a cut score of 1,150? If the best 10 students range from 1,000 to 1,100, those are the ones I'm going to admit. And if I have 20 applicants with scores above 1,300 why bother with anyone scoring 1,150?

As always, you can certainly use a combination of both methods. In the last example, you might set a cut score of 1,150 and if you don't get any applicants at least that high you'll just have empty classrooms that year; if you get enough candidates above that score, you'll rank them and admit the best. A final word of warning. Some people have suggested, as a sure way to avoid racial or other discrimination, to rank each group and hire a certain percentage. As law currently stands, you can't hire by quota. Another suggestion was to have different cut scores for each group so that the same proportion of each group was hired. Civil rights legislation has also made that illegal.

My suggestion: look at the situation carefully, and use a combination approach in most cases with the cut score *no higher than necessary*.

Don't Be Overprecise or Impractical!

There are no "exact sciences," but there are degrees of precision. And, frankly, psychology is not as precise, in most ways, as the physical sciences or even some of its biological cousins.

First, there's the precision of measurement. For example, to take a cognitive test score to the third decimal place doesn't mean much. If John is 115 on the IQ test and Frank is 116, don't expect to see much consistent difference in actual performance. For personality test measures, you may prefer to use "high, medium, and low!"

Next, there's the precision of terms. Intelligence is a broad term indeed, not nearly as precise as velocity. Some psychologists, attempting to emulate the more exact sciences, define terms with a high degree of exactness. For example, if I define intelligence as: "That score on the WAIS," then my measurement is as precise as the measure of velocity. But...it seems arbitrary.

Use the level of precision that fits your needs within the limits of your testing tools. Don't "split hairs" and don't make the mistake of not doing anything because you can't get absolute precision. A test may be imprecise, but an interview is even more so; and doing nothing is totally random!

Be Humble!

Tests, like all other selection devices, place people into categories. Tests, however, are seen as more precise, which they generally are, relative to other available selection devices. But, good though they are, they are far from perfect. Just because you have 15 personality measures and two cognitive test measures of Jim, don't think you have defined Jim as a person. He, like you and like me, is a totally unique being in the universe, and his personality and thinking style are not captured in 17 or 17 million numbers.

Developmental/Diagnostic

When people think of tests in the context of employment they usually think of devices to help decide to hire or not to hire. That's one use, but tests can and are used to help in the development of people, to know Jim's math ability to help direct him to the right training courses to increase that ability, and to know John's level of assertiveness to know if we need to provide him with assertiveness training.

As Jackson and Schuler (1990) point out, at times when labor pools shrink, employers must think more of training than selection. And tests can be a valuable tool in the training process.

Different Types of Users

The external consultant (e.g., an industrial psychologist contracted to do a specific project) may work with an internal consultant (e.g., the Human Resources Director) to provide information for decision makers (e.g., the Vice President of Sales). Each of these types of users needs to know the information discussed in this book, but while there are similarities in the needs of each type of test user, there are some substantial differences.

External Consultant

You are the person who makes the actual interpretation of the tests. Beware of being seen as an ivory tower intellectual with plenty of theory and no common sense; beware of being seen as a threat to the internal consultant discussed below.

1. *Know the organization!* Much of validity can generalize, especially in the area of cognitive tests. But that gives you no right to assume a "cookie cutter" approach. Know what the organization you advise *does* and what its people are like.

2. *Don't use jargon!* Of course, we have to have different terminology within any given field; that's to assist communication. Two psychologists talking about VPI "infrequency" know what that term means. But don't write a report in which you say, "Mr. Smith's infrequent vocational responses along with his careless/deviant responses to personality inventories..." That's jargon and it is not appropriate.

3. *Make recommendations carefully!* It's one thing to say, "Mr. Smith is extroverted," and another to say, "Mr. Smith is extroverted and will therefore be a good salesman." The first is an observation, the second is a conclusion that may not be warranted in every situation.

4. *Know the content of jobs!* I was talking with a young Ph.D. about the use of tests. She dismissed one test by saying, "It covers a lot of sales attributes but doesn't have much to do with management." She was astounded when I explained that the job of a good manager is largely sales, that most managers have sales-like personality traits, and that most top managers come from the sales ranks.

   For an overview, you can read the works of John Holland. Holland's theory groups jobs into six categories (e.g., sales and management are Enterprising jobs; accounting and budgeting are Conventional jobs) Read business books (such as Korn's *Success Profile*). Don't assume you know what traits match a given job until you've studied it in general, and in specific where possible.

5. *Be prompt!* Business is not an academic semester system. Days and hours count.

6. Don't write or say anything about a tested individual you wouldn't be willing to say to his/her face.

7. Remember that your recommendations affect people's lives. If a person is not hired who should be, the organization misses an opportunity and so does the individual. If a person is hired who should not be, the organization gets a bad apple and the person gets a failure experience.

8. *Know the tests!* Normal personality tests in particular have scale names that look obvious. Sociability is, after all, just plain old gregariousness or extraversion, right? No need to read the manual, examine the items, or look at past research, just tell how sociable the person is.

Ah, but...what do you do if the GZTS Social score is high, the VPI Social score is low, the GZTS Ascendance score is low, the NEO Agreeable score is midrange, and the VPI Enterprising score is high (a possible combination, believe me). Will you write: "She is very socially outgoing but not very socially oriented but certainly agreeable, timid and not socially bold she enjoys activities that allow her to be persuasive and directing in people situations." Think that's unlikely? Here's a report I actually generated from an interpretation system by a well-known scholar: "He rarely lets others take advantage of him and is very likely to put up with belligerence from others." Huh? People write such reports if they take scales at face value. The GZTS Social scale—a personality scale involving enjoyment of dealing with others—is correlated with the VPI Social scale, which is an interest scale involving liking for teaching and counseling jobs. But they do not mean the same thing. A person can be very outgoing in dealing with people but may not enjoy activities that involve teaching, training, or coaching.

Know your tests extremely well before you write (or say) a word about the results.

Internal Consultant

No one can be an expert in everything. The Human Resources (HR) function includes giving advice in wage and salary, hiring, advancement, promotion, and many other areas. Don't try to do it all yourself to the detriment of your organization.

1. Make sure testing is done by competent people! Many people who sell testing have no credentials. That will be a poor defense if your testing programs are challenged.

2. Make sure outside consultants really know the organization.

3. Make sure that reports, yours or those of outside consultants, are in plain English. If you hear "psychobabble" like "ego strength" or "ascendance," put a halt to it unless everyone in your company knows what those words mean. Neither should you allow someone to use business buzzwords like "dynamic" unless they have been defined.

4. Don't just "cover yourself." Human Resources people, like other staff functions, are often seen as the people who tell you what you can't do but not what you can do.

5. Never let outside consultants function as decision makers: They are there to give *advice*.

Decision Maker

You are the one who ultimately has the call on hiring, firing, and promotion. You are probably not an expert in testing, wage and salary, union-related law, and all those other areas. Your job is to run business and make use of the recommendations of experts.

1. *Don't accept jargon.* There is no concept in psychological testing that cannot be explained in plain English. If the consultant can't get terms into plain English—fast—find another consultant.

2. *Make sure the consultant knows the job.* Just that!

3. *Demand a fast turnaround.* Yes, the consultant needs to take the time to review tests carefully, but that should take hours, not weeks.

4. *Demand opinion.* Consultants, internal and external, are famous for giving you the 16 reasons why it just won't work. Don't allow it. If your Human Resources Director says a selection system isn't valid, demand one that is and evidence that it is. If a testing expert says Bill Smith wouldn't fit a sales job, ask what kind of job he would fit in.

5. *Don't just use a "thumbs up" approach.* In addition to making decisions about hiring, you can get information relevant to training, promotion, types of subordinates, co-workers, and superiors who will be most effective in dealing with this individual.

6. *Brush up on your interviewing!* The interview is a potentially flawed and discriminatory tool (see chapter 9), but it is one you must use from time to time.

7. *Don't delegate decision making!* It is *your* decision, period. Advice is just that. You, for example, must make the hiring decision regardless of what internal or external consultants tell you. Have some decision-making guidelines. Here is a suggested decision-making tool for hiring when using the advice of an outside consultant.

		Organization		
		Hire	Uncertain	Should not hire
	should hire	good bet	gamble	very risky
Consultant	uncertain	slight gamble	gamble	very risky
	should not hire	risky	very risky	very risky

good bet	All sources seem positive.
slight gamble	The consultant is uncertain, so there's a slight gamble—trust your judgment.
gamble	If you're uncertain, there's a gamble; hire if you need people, look at other candidates if you have the luxury of time and a large enough candidate pool.
risky	There are at least some negative opinions. Hire only if you can afford to take a risk.
very risky	There are too many negative opinions; don't hire. Notice that if you don't think you should hire it is very risky no matter what the outside consultant says.

Test Distortion Factors

Test Distortion and Parasitics

Tests are not given in the abstract. They are administered by people to people and even the best machines and computers have occasional problems in functioning. Let's keep in mind that every selection system is subject to distortion and then address testing.

Engineers, in building machines, deal with parasitics, the unwanted side effects of the system. A car engine heats up, even though that is not it's main function; in fact, the heat is the problem. Engineers try to cut down on these side effects. In some cases they are able to use the side effects (e.g., use the engine heat to heat the interior of the car during cold seasons).

Testing has it's share of parasitics. If you're assessing someone's personal traits you may not want to know about visual acuity or reading ability. In fact, they may only distort information. Some distortion factors:

Reading ability. If the test item says "I always endeavor to do a good job" you may get a misreading because the person does not understand the word endeavor.

Visual acuity. The person may have trouble with visual focus, especially for extended periods of time.

Second guessing. A person may go back and change his/her answers, ponder the meaning of a question before answering. In some cases the first response may be the most desirable.

Faking. A person may simply lie, especially on personality tests or integrity tests.

Fatigue. A person may become tired and inattentive with a long test.

Resentment. People may fail to cooperate with the testing process if they feel it is invasive or unnecessary. Employers, in turn, may hesitate to use potential good tests to avoid alienating future employees. Make the purpose of testing clear and, when at all possible, share as much of the testing results as possible.

Culture. A person from another country may be able to understand a test item yet not respond in our cultural context. In the United States a positive response to "I like the outdoors" may have a different connotation than to a person from Siberia.

Language. People who speak a foreign language well may have difficulty reading it, especially if it involves a different writing system. If the job does not require reading and writing, the test may impose an unfair burden. In addition, people may have cultural factors (see above) that are intertwined with language factors. To complicate the picture even more, even with fluency, people process information in ways that are very language-specific. A person with Spanish as her native language will probably think of medicine in English if taught in an American school. She may perform more poorly than her true ability if tested in Spanish.

Turnaround time. Some tests must be scored by testing companies and/or they must be clinically interpreted. That takes time, and in the business world the old saying "time is money" is quite true.

Jargon. If psychological terms are used, the end user may not understand. *Ascendance* and *ego strength* may not mean much to a business decision maker.

Contradiction. In an attempt to avoid jargon, some test users may use more everyday terms, and that can be a problem! It is possible that a person could score low on the VPI Soc scale and high on the Guilford Zimmerman Temperament scale. That combination of scores is quite meaningful. If you avoid lengthy descriptions and simply call both scales "social" you will have a report saying Jane Doe is very socially oriented but not very sociable. And that sounds very dumb.

Time decay. In general, test results are good over long periods of time because intelligence and personality tend to remain constant over time. Think of it as being like a photograph. If you are 40, you probably still resemble your high school annual picture. But not as much as you resemble the picture taken 2 years ago. In the same way, people can show changes in intellect and personality with the passage of time; usually gradual and small, in some cases quick and large.

Dealing With the Parasitics

It's best to keep the reading level of tests at a simple level. Second-guessing and faking are *not* such large problems in practicality (see discussion of faking in chapter 10 and the chapter 10 notes). Some tests can be administered orally, and this cuts down on problems of reading and visual acuity. Explaining the rationale for a test can cut down on resentment. People are more accepting of a spelling test if they know why spelling is important in the job. Keep the test battery as short as possible. It's not necessary to fatigue someone to get good information. Find ways to get scoring done on a timely basis. Avoid the use of jargon but don't simplify to the point of gaining apparent contradictions. Consult test manuals to see about time between re-test; in the absence of other information, I suggest you not use results that are over 2 years old.

In some cases you may want to make use of parasitics. If your math test requires an eighth grade reading level and the job also requires eighth grade reading level, your test may serve two functions.

STUDY QUESTIONS

- You have one test that measures speed of learning and another that measures persistence. Your research has shown that one ability can compensate for the other. For example, a person who learns slow but is persistent is often as good as a person who learns more quickly but is not as persistent. Should you use a multiple cutoff or additive method of test use?
- A clinical approach is always more accurate than a mere statistical or actuarial approach; true or false?

CHAPTER 6

COMMON EMPLOYMENT TESTS

- Cognitive tests measure learning and thinking ability.
- Normal personality tests which are not "projective" are most commonly used in industry.
- Interest tests can be useful.
- Tests can be standardized for a specific area of knowledge (e.g., licensing exams).
- Interviews and background data can be standardized and scored as tests.

Standard Tests

I may be a person who learns quickly or slowly: In other words, I have a certain *intellectual* ability (also called intelligence or cognitive ability). Regardless of my learning ability, I may be outgoing or shy, temperamental, or very consistent in my disposition: I have a certain *personality*. Regardless of those factors I may be interested in math or music: I have certain *interests*. And regardless of any of the others I may have a good understanding of nineteenth century German composers: I have certain *specific skills*.

Once you think of people in terms of their *intellect,* their *personality,*their *interests*, and their *specific knowledge* you can better understand the different types of tests. Cognitive tests look at intelligence factors. Personality tests look at the habitual ways that people act, (e.g., shy, outgoing or in-between, optimistic or pessimistic). Interest tests measure work interests. Some tests are specialized to measure specific skills in areas such as supervisory knowledge, and so forth.

Cognitive Tests

Tests that measure intellectual abilities are called *cognitive tests*. These include tests of basic intelligence, tests of reasoning ability, and tests of specific abilities such as math and vocabulary.

On the positive side, research has shown that cognitive tests tend to be highly intercorrelated (e.g., if you score high on a math test, you will probably score high on a general intelligence test). In addition, research shows that intellectual ability correlates positively with practically every kind of job. It may come as no big surprise, all things being equal, the smart person does better on any job than a person who is not as smart.

On the very bad side, cognitive tests will discriminate against minorities. Whites score higher than blacks on most cognitive tests. There were studies in the sixties and seventies that claimed the difference between whites and blacks was genetic, not social. The reason you haven't heard white racists making more of those studies is quite simple; research also shows that orientals score higher than whites!

We are all the same species, and if there are genetic differences that predispose a person with Japanese ancestry to learn more quickly than someone with German ancestry, they are likely small. We know for certain that people of every race have made contributions to art, science, and literature.

Nevertheless, as small or nonexistent as genetic differences may be, social class differences and attendant differences in opportunity have been very real and very large. Cognitive tests are effective at predicting performance and they do discriminate against blacks. Why? This subject is treated in more depth in chapter 10 and the notes for that chapter. If you plan to use cognitive tests you must read it.

Examples of cognitive tests

Wechsler Adult Intelligence Scale (WAIS). When psychologists use the term IQ they are generally referring to the intelligence quotient score on the Wechsler Adult Intelligence Scale. This test involves vocabulary, reasoning, memory, and so forth. It has a *verbal* section that involves the vocabulary tests and other such tests and a *performance* section that involves such tasks as putting blocks together to form a design.

Although the WAIS is an excellent test, it takes some time to give and it demands a trained administrator. In most employment settings, there are tests that can be group administered with no training on the part of the administrator. For example, the Wonderlic Personnel Test is much shorter and simpler to administer, and it correlates highly with the WAIS.

Wonderlic. This is a brief (12 minutes) timed test, which contains vocabulary, simple math problems, geometric designs—in short, it contains a wide range of cognitive problems. It has 16 different forms and a wide range of normative data. The manual reports score ranges for different positions and industries and lists many published studies. The Wonderlic is supported by various validity studies and also has convergent validity shown in its high correlation with the WAIS.

Pluses and minuses of cognitive tests

It may be a good idea to have a cognitive test in your testing battery. If it is a pass/fail hurdle in the procedure you almost certainly will discriminate against some minorities, and thus you must have a good reason for using the test. Be aware that this is still a hot area; while most psychologists are in agreement regarding the importance of intelligence, some people fear that the importance of cognitive tests is exaggerated, and their use is a way of hiding discrimination. See notes for this chapter and for chapter 10.

Clinical Personality Tests

Some people experience problems that require psychotherapy, medical treatment, and hospitalization. Clinical personality tests are designed to detect severe pathology in order to help direct the psychological and medical treatment that will be given. The best way to describe these tests is to describe an exemplary test, the MMPI.

Minnesota Multiphasic Personality Inventory (MMPI)

The MMPI is an empirically developed test, which contains scales such as Depression, Hysteria, Paranoia, and so forth. Originally developed in 1943, it has been revised (MMPI-2, 1989). There are various types of validity and lie scale scores. It is a well-researched instrument with clinical, configural, and actuarial prediction strategies. It is one of the most commonly used in clinical settings where psychologist and psychiatrists are treating mental problems. For industrial purposes, however, proceed with caution because it is probably not a good choice for most jobs. In addition, the MMPI items look like a test designed to find problems!

Pluses and minuses of clinical personality tests

There may be occasions in which there is a need to detect pathology. If someone is going to be the head of a nursery full of infants, it might be a good idea to detect pathology. Nevertheless, both ethically and legally, "invasion" is a function of the information gathered relative to a need to know. Many of the items on clinical personality tests sound weird, focusing on religion, sex, and waste elimination. You may have a need to use these tests, but be certain you are able to support that need with a great deal of evidence. Many industrial psychologists are not trained to use these instruments.

Normal Population Personality Tests

These are self-report tests that have primary application for the normal population. Instead of focusing on traits such as paranoia and depression, these tests look at sociability, activity level, attitude toward detail, and so forth. They overlap a great deal with the clinical tests but questions tend to be more obvious in content, and the information more applicable to job placement, than medical diagnosis.

Research has shown that most personality tests, especially those described in this section, have five major underlying factors. These five factors are: gregariousness or sociability, also called extraversion; neuroticism; interest in ideas; cooperativeness; conscientiousness. Sociability refers to the tendency of people to be outgoing, socially dominant, and enthusiastic as opposed to shy and passive. Neuroticism refers to being pessimistic, worried, depressed versus optimistic, happy, confident. Interest in ideas is an interest in thinking and learning and trying new ideas as opposed to being concerned only with practical, tried, and true. Cooperativeness refers to a desire to be pleasant and get along with people in a friendly and harmonious manner, turning the other cheek, and so forth versus being argumentative and hostile to people. Conscientiousness refers to having a strong work ethic and desire to do things right, according to some standard versus being lackadaisical and not always following through. A good example of this type of test is a relative newcomer, the NEO.

NEO

The NEO has five major factors, those described above. The factors of Neuroticism, Extraversion, and Openness are subdivided into several different areas, giving many different subscales. For example, extraversion is broken into gregariousness, assertiveness, activity and other facets. Two people may be equally extraverted, however, one may be more *outgoing* but less likely to be dominant than the other. The test is a relatively new one but shows a good deal of convergent validity with other more established tests. The items on the NEO generally have "face validity," that is, there are no strange items about religious beliefs or sexual fantasies.

The Guilford Zimmerman Temperament Survey (GZTS) and the 16PF

The GZTS has 10 major scales including G(general activity or energy level), R(restraint, or caution), A(ascendance or social dominance) S(sociability), and others. It has been used for years and is a well-researched scale. Hogan (1991) uses this test as an example of the predictive power of good personality tests in the business arena. The 16 PF is another well-known five-factor test. The scales are different than the GZTS, but, as Cattell, Eber, and Tatsuoka (1970, p. 44) point out, the two tests have very similar content but divide it up in different ways. They give statistical formulae for estimating the GZTS scales from the 16 PF scales.

Pluses and minuses of normal population personality tests

Even the normal population personality tests may look a bit odd to someone unaccustomed to taking them. Some tests contain a masculinity/femininity scale (for some reason), and many of those items seem (and in some cases are) unrelated to work. Whether someone wants to be a dress designer or a cowboy will probably distinguish between men and women (as if a test were needed to do that) but items about such issues are seldom job related and only reduce the perception of the test as a valid instrument.

Normal personality tests contain items whose content for the most part is fairly obvious. In theory, they are quite fakable: in practice, faking is not a problem. Personality tests provide good information but they are still far from perfect. For example, no matter how straightforward the information, there are combinations of score patterns, which require expert judgment. Consider the case of the Guilford Zimmerman Temperament Inventory, with its 10 different scales. If each scale were scored as high, medium, and low, there would be 59,000 combinations of scores—and there is no book that describes all 59,000 combinations. This means that clinical judgments must be made and those are difficult to validate.

Nevertheless, imperfect though they are, personality tests are extremely powerful. In chapter 10 and the related chapter notes we cover research showing that five factor tests, especially in the fields of sales and management, are very powerful. Management and executive success can be predicted years in advance using these tests. Although they must be interpreted by professionals, they can be administered, in many cases, with very little training.

Projective Personality Tests

These tests are not self-report in the usual sense. An example is the Rorschach. This test is a series of black-and-white and color inkblots. People look at these inkblots and tell what they look like.

At first glance, these tests often appear strange to nonpsychologists, the ultimate in psychological silliness. After all, since the inkblot is meaningless, how can a person's responses tell you anything?

According to the underlying theory, faced with an ambiguous situation the person projects his or her personality onto the situation. And that's not as wacky as it sounds!

What would you think if someone looked at 10 Rorschach inkblots (or cards or plates) and described each one as looking like some sex scene. Wouldn't you think he had sex on the brain? What if someone looked at the plates, (many of which research has shown usually elicit a sexual response), and described each one as looking like flowers. Wouldn't you think that person was being defensive? Even in cases that are not as extreme, responses can be interpreted. The Rorschach has years of research indicating what people usually say, what is a normal response (and some of those are about sex), and what is unusual.

Other projective techniques include the Thematic Apperception Test (TAT) in which there are pictures instead of inkblots—but the idea is the same. Some people use incomplete sentences. For example, you may have a sentence "It makes me feel angry when _____" and let the person complete the sentence. If you have someone who completes the sentence "—when the worthless commies put electronic bugs in my house" you might suspect the person's thinking was a bit unusual. And, as with the other projective techniques, some incomplete sentence tests have research that shows what is or is not an unusual response.

Pluses and minuses of projective personality tests

Hogan (1991) shows some cases in which projective tests work in industrial settings. But, these tests appear less straightforward to the layperson and may arouse anxiety, suspicion, and skepticism. They must be administered by professionals. If a projective technique is the best and most cost-effective, you may elect to use it. A suggestion: try to gain the same information with more direct self-report measures.

Integrity Tests

A special subset of personality tests are those that attempt to measure honesty or integrity (e.g., is this a person who will steal, use drugs at work?) These tests are discussed in chapter 9 and again in chapter 10.

Vocational Interest Tests

These tests do not assess ability or personality, but they do assess interest in different occupations. Because they do not assess ability—and are not designed to do so—they are not always used in selection.

On the other hand, for some jobs it could be argued that an interest in the work is important. For example, if a person has a low interest in sales work, he/she might not stay for long in a high-pressure sales job. In addition, the work of John Holland has shown that work interests are consistently related to personality factors. People who are interested in sales jobs tend to be energetic and extraverted people. People interested in mechanical, blue-collar, and labor-type jobs tend to be more introverted.

Finally, we must not forget that *selection* is only one function of employment testing. Employers may use interest tests to help employees develop their own skills and abilities. Let's look at two vocational interest tests: the Vocational Preference Inventory (VPI) and the Strong Campbell Interest Inventory (SCII).

VPI and SCII

Both of these instruments gain information about work interests. The Strong Campbell Interest Inventory is a lengthy, in-depth test instrument, the descendant of one of the earliest empirically keyed interest inventories. The Vocational Preference Inventory, a much shorter test, is one of several instruments created by John Holland based on his theory of vocational personality types. Holland (see Holland, 1992, for the latest version of a much-reprinted book) cogently argues that vocational preference and personality are closely related. The theory has many implications (e.g., people with certain personalities are more congruent [compatible] with some types of jobs than others). So powerful is his theory that the SCII was adapted to conform to Holland theory. The SCII and VPI and the Self-Directed Search (another Holland test) give different types of information, but all three give information about the individual in terms of his/her interests in physical labor (Realistic), science (Investigative), creative work (Artistic), coaching and training (Social), management, sales, and persuasion (Enterprising), and business systems (Conventional).

Pluses and minuses of interest tests

Interest tests are very valuable but should be used in conjunction with other tests in making selection decisions. They have the value of being straightforward and gaining good personality information without being invasive or anxiety provoking.

Special Knowledge Tests

Any teacher develops several specialized knowledge tests every semester. If there is a large enough group that takes the same type of test, it is a good idea to make it more sophisticated and consistent. So, for example, professionals like accountants, physicians, and psychologists often taken standardized tests of specialized knowledge.

Knowledge tests often overlap with cognitive tests. For example, a test of use of fractions is a special type of knowledge but shares a g factor and will be correlated with general intelligence tests.

Special Tests

Structured Interviews

See chapter 9 for a discussion of the pitfalls of the interview and some suggestions for doing a good interview. Interviews become more valid as they become more structured...that is, as they become more like standardized tests. Interviews, despite their problems WILL be used in the business world. Make sure you use them for the right reasons, not because they are more legal (they are not), more valid (they are less valid) or less discriminatory (they are more likely to be discriminatory).

Biodata

By scoring and weighting an application blank you can turn it into a test. For example, research may show that years of experience in carpentry and education beyond high school can be weighted and added to predict job success in certain craft positions. There are several problems. First, you must be careful to avoid asking discriminatory questions. Length of time at present residence may predict something, but the EEOC will probably find it unfair if challenged. Some types of biodata could change in effectiveness with time. Biodata can be very useful, but use it with care.

Overview

There are many different types of tests. Choose your test battery carefully and make sure it fits your unique needs. Don't let legal concerns be your only concern, but try to stay within reasonable bounds. Think in terms of *respect* to the test-taker and *relevance* to the job.

STUDY QUESTIONS

- Is the WAIS a personality test?
- Can anyone administer most projective tests?
- Is it relatively easy to administer most normal personality tests?

CHAPTER 7

TESTING PROGRAMS—IDEAL AND REAL

- In the ideal world you have access to large samples, solid criteria, and unlimited time.
- Real world companies seldom approximate the textbook validation world.
- Even in the real, imperfect world there are good ways to approach testing programs!

We have looked at test development and test usage. Let's see how you would actually implement a testing program, starting with a very ideal situation. In most cases this ideal situation will, in fact, not be obtained. But it's worth looking at how it should be done if it only could.

In the Ideal World

You're going to develop a test for machinists at Big Machine Company. You carefully study the job with the assistance of some industrial engineers and determine that the job involves using addition, subtraction, multiplication, and division using whole numbers, decimals, and fractions. In addition, people must be able to handle the stress of a great deal of noise and rapidly changing schedules. There is a stress on teamwork, so people must cooperate. Those factors account for 99% of the job variance.

You choose two math tests, a stress reaction test and a scale on teamwork from standardized test. These four measures serve as your initial test battery. The tests have good previous research backing them.

BMC has a group of 280 machinists, with about equal numbers of black men, white men, black women, and white women. Blacks and whites are the only racial/ethnic groups in the work area. The company agrees to let you test all 280 machinists and keep the results of that testing 100% confidential. They supply you with performance ratings on the 280 machinists, performance ratings given by supervisors who have been thoroughly trained in a performance review system that is very exact.

You place all 280 people into a vast room with good lighting and ventilation. You and 10 test proctors administer your tests, checking each man and woman's identity badge against the name preprinted on the test. During the test you make sure there is no cheating or talking. The tests are gathered up and scored.

You randomly sample 140 of the tests and correlate them with the performance data. You find that the math tests and personality test subscales in a multiple regression equation correlate significantly with performance, but the stress test seems to add very little. Math Test #1 discriminates against black women. When you remove it, the overall prediction is negligibly affected and the discrimination goes away. You cross-validate your results on the other 140 sets of test data and confirm your original formula. Even with "shrinkage" taken into account the results are impressive.

The company agrees to use your test battery for a couple of years without seeing the results. This will allow you to gather information about how effective the tests would be (if used) but without restricting range. The company will continue to hire people based on their interviews and reference checks, but they won't use the tests or even know the data—that all goes to you. You continue to give the stress test, even though it didn't show any positive correlation. Perhaps the stress test results predicts behavior that doesn't show up for some years in the future.

The company also agrees to let you review all performance measures to make sure they are as accurate and objective as possible. After 2 years, you have performance ratings on the 280 people in the original group plus ratings on the 280 people who have been hired since then. Once again, you do a statistical analysis. Your math test continues to work, the personality subscale is even more positive across time, and the stress test shows a slight but significant addition. After making some minor revisions, you put together the testing program. You supply the tests to be used, the manner in which they are to be administered and scored, and the revised formula for combining the test scores to make a decision about hiring. The company contracts you to revisit every 2 years to update the information. There appears to be no discriminatory impact on people as a function of age, race, or gender.

After another 3 years, 1 year's data shows an adverse impact on blacks. Nevertheless, your tests are all solidly job related so you know you will win if taken to court. And since Big Machine is known for nondiscrimination and valid tests, attorneys are not likely to take things to court.

Are there companies that do their validation in that manner for some positions? Some probably come close. Are there companies that do their validation in that manner for every position in the company? I'll wager there's never been one in the history of the world. Do *most* companies have the numbers of people to do such a study even if it were economically feasible? Absolutely not.

In the Real World #1

Widget Incorporated wants to give some tests to get better people. The VP of Administration calls you in. She has to fill 17 programmer slots in the next month and doesn't want to rely on an interview. Widget needs a programmer test battery. She has 20 programmers on board.

Well, clearly you don't have enough people to do any sort of statistics, so forget all that stuff you learned in tests and measurements. Nice idea, but it doesn't fit Widget MIS Department. Throw away the textbook and get on with the real world.

You confer with the VP. She personally feels that graphology is important, so you find a test in a graphology book. There's also a color preference test that people at her church used, and it told a lot. You know that the MMPI is a good test. You give all of the current group of 20 programmers the test battery. The VP doesn't really know the programmers, except for one who's a friend. She interviews the group for 15 minutes and makes some performance evaluations based on that. She would like to avoid hiring hispanics like Raul in the future. (Not prejudiced mind you, hispanics just don't pay attention to detail.) You look at the data. Mary, the friend, likes the colors red and blue. Some of the "poor" performers (based on the 15-minute interview) answer yes to some of the standardized test questions about hair on their bodies. You and the VP agree that you need to keep track of who tends to be a "homo," so you need some questions about those areas. Oh, yes. The VP has observed that people who like gothic novels are the ones who always get emotional when criticized.

Final test? A hundred-item test containing color preference items, a graphology section, two questions about body hair, some questions about sex, and a question about preference for gothic novels over football. Based on that score, the VP eliminates 90% of the applicants and interviews the remainder, especially careful to watch shifting eye contact.

In the Real World #2

Smith, Smith, and Smith (3S), a growing snack food company, is going to hire 10 regional managers. They have five on board. You can't find any data on regional managers—much less those in snack foods—for any standardized test.

Corporate counsel sympathizes with your desire for some testing and screening tools but points out that a) you don't have, nor ever will have, a sufficient sample to validate any test and b) you would have to generalize from other management positions to use any other test. He tells you to forget testing and just rely on your gut feel in the interview. Especially note the handshake—a good firm one is a salesman, every time.

In the Real World #3

Momenpop Trucking needs a test for truck drivers. They need it now. They currently have 20 drivers, and they want to hire an additional 15 within the next 9 months, and they're tired of hiring based on "good old boy" interviews.

There's a small sample of people and there are little or no recorded performance data. You clearly don't have that ideal world you read about in the textbook. But you aren't discarding everything you've learned. You are going to design a selection system that is as good as you can make it.

President Sam Momenpop and his top staff say the job demands the ability to learn, read, write, and do basic math. They want people who show up for work and don't mind the stress of long hours, rapidly changing priorities, and argumentative customers. That seems consistent with the tasks involved.

The job is somewhat specialized; it's not just truck driving. Drivers not only drive the load of prefab commercial structures, they also help in set-up once they get there and frequently trouble-shoot customer problems. There's no standard test battery for this position.

You examine several tests. The quick intelligence test is one with years of research. The items are math, vocabulary, and general reasoning. There are no history items that would be biased against someone from another country. There are no "church is where you have to be quiet" items that would be subtly biased against different religious sects. The test is used for many other types of labor, and it correlates well with various performance measures.

One test of "work ethic" has various studies showing correlations with performance data, but the items are strange. One of them says: "I believe that God talks to me." Regardless of how that item is scored, it seems invasive to you. You pass on that test. The next test you examine hasn't been used with truck drivers, but it has been used in many other types of jobs, and it correlates with measures such as punctuality. The items are very direct and seem content valid—"I think it's important to abide by company policy."

The stress tolerance scale is new, redesigned to avoid EEOC and ADA concerns. The items look good. There is no direct correlation of the test with a criterion, but it correlates well with other well-established stress tests. You decide to take a chance on construct and content validity because you don't want the risk of some of the physical-health items on other stress tests.

You now have your test battery. You still want to see how people actually score, even though your sample of 20 people is too small for practical purposes.

You test the on-board people even though the tests have to be taken in the field unmonitored; Momenpop can't lose the thousands of dollars involved in bringing everyone into the office. You attempt to gain at least some criterion data by getting the officers to rank people on an overall 1 (this person meets all of our standards and we would hire him/her again) to 3 (this person is about to be fired for cause) rating scale. There aren't many 3s, and two of those get fired before completing the tests. You don't really get much in the way of statistical significance—with that sample size and range restriction you didn't expect to do so.

You set a cut score that would exclude only 20% of the group. The "1s" and most of the "2s" score higher than three of the four "3s" who managed to complete the test before being fired.

Over the next few years you do your best to introduce a new performance rating system including on-time delivery, customer rating and overall performance in five areas. After 2 years, 78 applicants have been tested and 28 have been hired. Of course, the range of those 28 scores is restricted since people are hired only if they pass an interview and the test. One person who marginally passes is rated quite well; of course, he's the son of a major client. You are initially shocked to find that some high-scoring people have had problems with on-time delivery. But Sam tells you that it's no big surprise; he gave those good scorers some of the oldest trucks and toughest routes, and they're doing great.

Momenpop Company is convinced that the testing program contributes to getting a better class of people. As per your recommendation, the company is also using interview training to improve the interview portion, and they are checking references more consistently. "Besides," says the President, "the testing keeps supervisors on their toes. If they interview a person and say he's great, they get embarrassed if that person later fails the tests. And even though I know they're still as prejudiced as they ever were, when black applicants score well, they can't use the old `bad attitude in the interview' excuse."

So, What's Best in an Imperfect World?

The ideal world is best, of course. If you live in Idealworld, you have it knocked. Give any graduate student a textbook and he or she can knock out your validation study.

If you don't live in Idealworld—and it's 95% probable that you don't—you probably work with or for companies like Widget, 3S, or Momenpop. Some real similarities in those three cases. And all the difference in the world.

Similarities: Momenpop, 3S, and Widget are like most businesses—small and tight with their budgets. They are unsophisticated with regard to selection, they do not have hundreds of people in each job nor the willingness to suspend business operation while an experiment is being performed. While their jobs are like other jobs, they are rarely *exactly* alike. And decision makers in various departments do NOT have to follow the dictates of the VP of Human Resources much less the outside expert. In fact, in the feudalistic society that is modern business, even presidents and chairmen do not manage by edict as much as the nonbusiness world imagines.

Differences: Widget took a bad situation and made it even worse. Using the excuse that they couldn't do a sophisticated validation, they violated the rules of common sense and basic ethics and did something sloppy and discriminatory. Take a stroll down selection lane in many companies and you'll find, unfortunately, widget-like nonsense: like a real-life nonhypothetical HR Director (an attorney by the way) who told me that testing was only an adjunct to his ability to look at the eye movements of a candidate to determine integrity.

The case of 3S is interesting because their stance seems reasonable—don't test. Unfortunately, legal counsel didn't do his homework or he would have discovered that the "gut feel" interview *is* a test and *has* been tried and found wanting as such.

Momenpop didn't do it by the book, but they came as close as they could. The measures they used made good common sense. They tried to avoid being unfair or unnecessarily invasive. They examined the effect the testing was having on the actual hiring process. Unless someone wants to give a multimillion dollar grant to Momenpop there's simply no way for them to do the textbook validation. But the system they have *now* is better than the inconsistent and totally subjective system they had before.

It's not easy to do a Momenpop study, but that's the best most businesses can do, and that's infinitely better than Widget and considerably better than 3S.

CHAPTER 8

LEGAL ISSUES

- EEOC and relevant law is far different than many people imagine.
- You can't play it safe! Everything is a test, and all aspects of employment have liabilities.
- There are things you can do to try and stay out of court.

Testing affects the lives of people, especially in employment settings. It affects the individual who may or may not get a job depending on test score. It affects the business owner who may hire the wrong people. Therefore, it is—and should be—governed by legal guidelines. Many people imagine they understand these legal issues and practically no one does. Please read this chapter carefully, it may surprise you.

EEOC

The Equal Employment Opportunity Commission enforces many of the laws involving hiring and other personnel actions, especially Title VII (which prohibits discrimination by race, color, religion, sex or national origin) and other acts (e.g., Age Discrimination in Employment Act of 1967, amended in 1978 and 1986, prohibits discrimination against people over 40). The EEOC will direct you to The Uniform Guidelines of 1978. The Uniform Guidelines contain the position of the Equal Employment Opportunity Commission relative to hiring. There is a lot of fine print, and most people choose not to read the Uniform Guidelines first-hand. And by the time the information gets filtered through several sources, it can seem that the Uniform Guidelines are antibusiness, draconian rules that demand you hire on a racial basis regardless of business need. Nothing could be further from the truth. Get a copy of these guidelines and read them, fine print and all. If you still have questions, contact an attorney knowledgeable in labor and employment law. But before we get into the nuts-and-bolts of the various sections let's look at how eminently reasonable the Uniform Guidelines are in spirit.

Understanding the Spirit of EEOC

In thumbnail sketch form, this is what the Guidelines say: If you do not discriminate against a racial, ethnic or gender group, EEOC doesn't care what you do. The commission is not there to meddle in business.

If you *do* discriminate against a racial, ethnic, or gender group, even that may be acceptable! As long as you can show that the selection procedure you used was a business necessity. You are not expected to harm your business or your clients. It's not designed to be an unfair system.

Suppose you're staffing a cardiac hospital. You don't hire any white heart surgeons. If challenged, you may be asked to demonstrate *why* that happened. If you show that no whites passed your test of heart surgery ability you must then show that your test was a reasonable measure of heart surgery success. You must also show that your test of heart surgery did not cover information that could be easily taught. And if you can show that, that's the end of the issue. You can use your test, even if it does lead to low levels of hiring whites.

The spirit of EEOC is to keep the employer from excluding people from jobs based on blatant racial policy or hiding prejudice behind a selection procedure that looks innocent.

Here are some pertinent EEOC issues you should be aware of:

The Guidelines are Guidelines

Even if you don't follow the guidelines slavishly you may have a valid test. The Uniform Guidelines are intended to be *guidelines*. Having said that, it's a good idea to know them and attempt to follow them.

Organization size. As Arvey (1988) discusses, Title VII applies to all employers with more than 15 employees (many businesses have less).

Definition of selection procedure. (UG, §16Q) "Any measure, combination of measures, or procedure used as a basis for any employment decision. Selection procedures include the full range of assessment techniques from traditional paper and pencil tests, performance tests, training programs, or probationary periods and physical, educational, and work experience requirements through informal or casual interviews and unscored application forms." Remember—everything's a test!

When the EEOC expects validation. (UG, §1B) "These guidelines do not require a user to conduct validity studies of selection procedures where no adverse impact results." That is a very good general guideline, if you read it as saying, "if you keep your numbers straight you'll probably not be challenged"—do NOT read this as saying you are permitted to keep your numbers straight by any method, as we'll discuss below. You can't hurt people in order to keep a good bottom line.

Adverse impact. This is a difference in the rate at which a minority group is hired versus the majority group. What is a difference? Uniform Guidelines, §4D points out that adverse impact can be any difference that is "significant in statistical and practical terms" (see the chapter on statistics) or where the use of the selection procedure discourages minority application. As a guideline, the Uniform Guidelines use a "four-fifths rule" which means the minority group hiring rate is less than 80% of the majority hiring rate. So, if you hire 50 of every 100 white applicants and 40 of every 100 black applicants you're right on the borderline.

Challenge of adverse impact. If the plaintiff can show adverse impact, that is, that minorities were hired at a substantially lower rate than the majority, the burden of proof shifts to the employer. The employer must prove that its selection procedure was valid, that is, that the selection procedures were related to a sound business-related criterion.

The aspects of selection likely to be challenged. It is the overall selection process that is important. Uniform Guidelines, §4C states, "If this information shows that the total selection process does not have an adverse impact the Federal Employment Agencies, in the exercise of their administrative and prosecutorial discretion, in usual circumstances, will not expect a user to evaluate the individual components for adverse impact or to validate such components and will not take any enforcement action based upon the adverse impact of any component of that process, including the separate parts of a multipart selection procedure or any separate procedure that is used as an alternative method of selection." In short, if the XYZ test discriminates in favor of whites but other good measures balance out, the company is probably not in trouble—there's the good news. Here's the bad news—if the company spends $400,000 to validate the math test but the interviewers discriminate against Hispanics, your valid test means nothing. Also, watch out for one component of testing being an absolute hurdle. Read about "staying out of court."

Race norming. The Civil Rights Act of 1991 did away with race norming. You can't adjust your hiring rates of minorities or other protected groups by using different cut scores.

"It shall be an unlawful employment practice for the respondent, in connection with the selection or referral of applicants or candidates for employment or promotion, to adjust the scores of, use different cut-off scores for, or otherwise alter the results of employment-related tests on the basis of race, color, religion, sex, or national origin." (See §106 of The Civil Rights Act of 1991.)

Things you probably shouldn't include in a test. There are some items that should usually be omitted from an application blank (which is, of course, a test). Items that are questionable are those that directly address race, gender, ethnicity, or socioeconomic status, for example. Check with your local EEOC office for a list of items.

You should also consider the items and scales of a test and the items they contain. For example, some tests contain a masculinity/femininity scale. Even if you did a study and found a strong relationship between the masculine pole of the scale and success on the job I would suggest you not use it. You could perhaps make a strong case, but this scale *would* discriminate against women—by design—and there's probably nothing it measures you couldn't measure some other way.

Testing for promotion. Standardized testing may not be appropriate in some promotion situations because the individual is on board and has had a chance to show a track record. If Tom does a good job welding and you need a welder class II, why give a test and guess? He's already proven himself with action.

Nevertheless, if there is a big change in job duty (e.g., moving into a management role) testing may be involved. Just remember that the Uniform Guidelines do not look only at hiring but at all employment decisions.

Office of Federal Contract Compliance (OFCC)

The OFCC enforces an executive order quite similar to title VII that applies to companies that serve as contractors or subcontractors on government jobs.

Americans With Disabilities Act (ADA)

In July of 1992, the ADA went into effect. It may be the most sweeping civil rights law ever enacted. It affects all aspects of life. With regard to employment, it became effective for employers with over 25 employees on July 26, 1992; for employers with 15–24 employees the effective date is July 26, 1994. (Remember that ADA does not apply to many businesses, those with fewer than 15 people.)

With regard to employment, no employer may require a pre-employment medical examination except for drug screening. (An exam may be required *after* a job offer.) Is a written test a medical examination? In most cases the answer would seem to be no, but some neuropsychogical exams might arguably be classed as "medical." Employers are not allowed to ask about physical limitations nor past alcohol or drug usage. They can only look at ability to do the job. Are physical ability items on a test covered by the same guidelines? If an item on a test says, "I enjoy sports" the item is probably not intended to measure sports or physical ability but is rather an indirect measure of enthusiasm, energy, and so forth. Nevertheless, it covers physical activity and implicitly physical ability. How will law evolve? As one attorney discussing ADA pointed out in the summer of 1991, "...there are no assurances as to how courts will ultimately view a particular inquiry or that the law as presently constituted will not change." (Finlayson, 1991). It's a good idea for any test user to monitor developments in this area because it is still in a state of flux and may be for many years to come.

Affirmative Action

Many people are confused by "Affirmative Action" because it sounds like reverse discrimination, and it can become that if employers are not careful! Affirmative action plans show a preference for a particular group in order to balance past injustices. Affirmative action programs are very good in theory, but in practice they can create problems. As in so many other cases, there are no easy answers. Affirmative action affects all aspects of selection, so always advise businesses to adhere to the four points below.

Affirmative action programs must be:

1. Remedial of an imbalance due to past hiring practices.

2. Temporary, dismantled when the goals are met.

3. Fair to other groups (e.g., you can't fire 10 white employees in order to hire 10 black).

4. One factor but not an "absolute bar" to other groups.

Unions

When dealing with union employees, there are certainly situations where you can use testing, but you need to be aware of specific laws and agreements that may impact that use. These can differ from situation to situation.

Other Laws

The laws of your state or those that govern your industry may affect selection procedures. Be aware of them in using testing or any other selection procedure. Consult an attorney who is expert in labor and employment law—preferably in a well-known firm—but be sure the attorney knows at least as much about testing as this book covers. If you anticipate going to court, contact the EEOC office to get appropriate materials regarding the Civil Rights Act of 1991.

Why You Can't "Play It Safe"

You Can't Protect Yourself With Empty Files!

Of course you can't, so why state the obvious? Because people actually say "we won't put anything in our files about selection, so no one can show we did anything wrong." Not only is that not a *defense* in the case of adverse impact or some other legal hassle, courts might see it as an admission of guilt. You can, in fact, run into a "Catch-22" situation. In order to make sure you are not discriminating, you will probably want to keep track of race and gender of applicants. Yet, if challenged, you must make sure that people did not use that information to make hiring judgments! Some companies use a "tear sheet" method in which information about race and gender (age, etc.) is completed and then torn from the application and put in a separate file.

There's No "Grandfather Clause!"

It doesn't matter when the test was made or the selection procedure was implemented, you have to abide by the law as it is now.

Anyone Can Sue You!

They may or may not have a sound case, but they can certainly make your life miserable while you prove you didn't discriminate. People may choose to use the testing portion of a selection system as a scapegoat. There's no way to be sure this won't happen with a test or any other selection instrument.

Negligent Hiring and Respondeat Superior

Oh, this whole business of hiring is a hassle! Tests are liable, interviews are tests, employees can sue, bringing class action suits. Why not be lax in your hiring standards and just hire whoever shows up until the jobs are filled? Ask the minimum job-related questions and hire them.

Bad idea. Besides the obvious problems of reducing quality of work output you still have problems with legal issues.

You see, you not only have an obligation to be fair to job candidates, you also have an obligation to anyone that your employees come in contact with.

Let's say that, in order to avoid hassles you hire Joe Doe. No test, scant interview, no reference check, bare bones application blank, he can operate the forklift, hire him. Then he shows up at work drunk, and hits someone with the forklift—and your company is liable.

You hire an apartment manager. No invasive tests! Don't check references! No background check! Play it safe. Then he rapes one of the tenants. Once the trial takes place, expert witnesses testify to his psychopathic traits and his history of violence. The court wonders why you made no attempt to determine the qualities of a person in such a sensitive position. You have no answer. And you are liable beyond your reckoning. Ethically as well as legally.

Fairness May Demand Thoroughness

Ah, says the Director of HR. I'll play it safe by making a selection procedure that contains only the most concrete aspects of the job, and leave out all of the abstract issues such as "motivation" and "leadership." One city attempted to defend its firefighter promotion test and the courts nevertheless found the test inappropriate. Because it asked too much? No! Because it did not ask enough! It did not cover supervisory ability and the court said such ability was obviously a component of the job (*Firefighters Institute of the City of St. Louis*, 1976).

Hiring is Not the Only Area of Liability

It's not just the way you hire; it starts with how you recruit. But, even after hiring, do you imagine that if you just hire with no hassles your legal liability is over? EEOC applies to promotion and wrongful discharge as much and sometimes more than hiring. In 1990, hiring claims amounted to less than 9% and promotion and wrongful discharge over 60%. If you don't hire carefully, you may have trouble promoting or even keeping people. And don't forget the area of negligent hiring that begins after you hire.

The Interview is Not a Safe Alternative to Testing

Read chapter 9! The interview is a test in EEOC terms, and it has all of the problems of standardized testing—and more.

"Doing Nothing" is Not a Safe Alternative to Testing

Read chapter 9! Anything you do to hire is a test. Anything you *don't* do is a lack of defense against negligent hiring claims.

The Experts Don't Agree

Test experts, business managers, EEOC Guidelines, and court rulings: Sometimes they agree and sometimes they don't. And there is not one "right" camp to be in. The courts expect you to use common sense. If slavish adherence to the Uniform Guidelines leads to a bad decision (see the section on negligent hiring) you can't argue that you did the wrong thing in order to be safe.

You Can't Discriminate Against One Group to be Fair to Another

There is an emphasis on "keeping your numbers straight" implicit in the EEOC guidelines. Some people may misinterpret this as meaning you need only show preferential treatment of women and minorities and hire a certain quota. Wrong! The EEOC wants to protect *every* group—minority or majority. In addition, while EEOC protects groups, blatant discrimination against individuals to achieve group parity is not acceptable.

Some Final Thoughts on Playing it Safe

As a wise man once said, "Avoiding legal liability in business is like putting a queen size sheet on a king size bed. Something is going to be uncovered." If you pay attention to protecting fellow employees, your business, and your clients, you will err in the direction of being unfairly tight in hiring. If you go out of your way to be easy and nondemanding with every job candidate you will suffer a loss in quality and run the risk of negligent hiring. Make some business decisions, use good reasoning, and balance your risk positions.

Some Thoughts on Staying Out of Court

While you must give up the idea of "playing it safe" you can "play it as safe as possible." In today's litigious society some people take the dismal view that it isn't IF you will get sued—it's when. It's still a good idea to try to stay out of court, because it will cost you, even if you win. Here are some guidelines:

1. *At the risk of stating the obvious—don't discriminate!* Sure, there are some companies that get away with blatant discrimination. There are some who try their best to be fair and get hung out to dry on a technicality. Overall, however, people who try to do the right thing are less likely to get sued.

   Try to keep your numbers straight, keeping low or no adverse impact and abide by ADA. You may show a preference for a racial group or gender, all other factors being equal, in order to remedy past discrimination (see Affirmative Action).

   The greater your adverse impact the more validation evidence you will need. You may find, for example, that rather than excluding minorities who do not pass your test of basic math you can instead introduce your own in-house training program. Your test of basic math can be a training diagnostic rather than a device to exclude. However you do it, do the best you can to avoid discrimination.

2. *Avoid waving a red flag.*

   In theory you can ask anything or test anything that is job related. Can you ask about religion? Sure you can, if you're hiring a Rabbi to oversee Kosher in your plant! But in most cases, practically speaking, if you ask about height, marital status, and so forth, you are waving a red flag even if you *can* show that these factors are job related.

3. *Show good intentions.*

   Some attorneys will tell you that, in the law, results matter, not intentions. Theoretically this is right. But judges and juries are human beings, and good intentions often matter to human beings, whatever they may say. So, make a nondiscriminatory message part of your company culture, put it in the handbook, *preach it.* Explain to people *why* you are giving tests, why you need information on an application blank, and why you ask the things you ask in an interview.

4. *Be respectful.*

   Make sure you present tests to the applicants in the most respectful manner possible. Lawsuits have been triggered by people telling a woman, "Hey we never hire women." Say dumb things like that and you'll end up in court. Make sure that your company representatives are respectful at every step of the selection process!

5. *Make sure YOU know why you're using any selection instrument.*

The courts have been quite understanding when there are good reasons for tests, interviews, experience requirements, and so forth. But don't be careless!

- Don't require "2-years experience" unless you need it.
- Don't require passing a test of math ability for someone who won't be doing math.
- Don't require a test of leadership for people who won't be leading.

If you require passing a well-designed test of "cooperativeness" for people who are going to be part of an emergency medical team, you can probably make a strong argument that lack of cooperation can lead to death of a patient. If you require passing a test of sociability for sales professionals, you should be able to marshall evidence for the dreadful economic impact of hiring ineffective sales people, and an introverted sales staff will almost certainly be ineffective. If you require passing a test of mental stability for people working in routine clerical positions with no public contact, your test may be seen as arbitrary.

6. *Make sure you explain to applicants why you are using the tests.*

Applicants have a right to know that employers are not capriciously giving them tests. People who initiate court cases are usually those who feel that they have been treated unfairly .

7. *Try to avoid using tests with wacky-sounding items.*

In the first place, it may be illegal in some cases. In any event it makes the test-taker angry. And if it goes to court, the attorney will love funny-sounding items to read aloud. If there is a very good reason to ask questions about religion or sex, you may want to do it, but it needs to be a *very* good reason. As one attorney put it: "Just as tests and validation studies marked by obvious signs of common sense are less likely to be challenged, those marked by obvious lack of common sense are more likely to be challenged" (Seymour, 1988).

8. *Monitor the effects of testing.*

If you have adverse impact against 50 people for 1 year, that's bad. If you have adverse impact against 500 for 10 years , that's VERY bad.

9. *Be careful with "pass/fail" hurdles or single selection components that have a major effect.*

There are some situations in which one factor or ability is key. On one hand it may seem silly to waste your time or that of the candidate's if he/she fails one crucial component of a selection process. Why give ten more tests when the person has already failed one that is critical? But temper that decision with this fact: Any selection component that is a pass/fail hurdle is more liable to be examined and found wanting than one which is used in an overall context. As you can read in the chapter notes, in *Connecticut v. Teal*

(1982), one of the problems seemed to be the fact that one selection component eliminated people from passing other tests. Even though there is no overall "four-fifths" impact, where one selection component has an absolute or even major effect on further consideration of one subgroup, it may be challenged.

This is NOT to say that single component hurdles should not be used. Don't hire clumsy brain surgeons even if they have good clinical knowledge and excellent bedside manner. Don't hire racially prejudiced police officers even if they have excellent skills as marksmen and thorough knowledge of the law. Don't hire salesmen who don't like dealing with people. Don't hire blind airline pilots.

10. *Know your test history.*

Attorneys are more likely to litigate when the tests being used have been condemned previously in courts. If the ABC test is the best for your job, use it even if court cases have found its use inappropriate in other settings. But use something else if you have a choice.

11. *Know attorney motivations.*

Attorneys like public accolades as much as academics like publications and politicians like favorable endorsements. If your situation is one that is likely to establish some new precedent, be aware that it is more attractive to attorneys.

12. *If you can do a good criterion-validity study, by all means do it.*

If you have a very large sample of people with a very sound criterion, then by all means do the statistical analysis and make any changes necessary to make your procedure even more valid. Don't do a study with 30 people and start demanding, based on the results, that all salesmen be slow paced or that all accountants should be sloppy or that you can exclude blacks because of "business necessity." Use common sense and don't think a small study will allow you to violate personal rights or business sense and get away with it.

13. *Use common sense!*

If you use a color coding test because your wife's uncle said it helped his cousin Joe hire salesmen, that's not a defense. If one of your managers tells people, "You can take the test, but I warn you, Mexicans don't do very well," then you may end up in court before you wise up and fire the manager. If you have 10 people interviewing with no interview training or interview guidelines, you are using a *test that is not valid* and, moreover, could not possibly be validated. If you give people a battery of tests with strange items about their urine and don't give any explanation as to *why* you gave the tests, you may irritate people enough to sue you. If you make an arbitrary test requirement based on a "criterion valid" study with 35 people measured against a criterion of "customer satisfaction" as measured by vague opinions, that requirement will *not* be considered empirically valid.

Choose tests (and interviews and application blanks) with care and examine them relative to your jobs. Demand that the tests (and interviews and application blanks) be administered consistently and with respect to every job applicant. Monitor procedures to see that blatant discrimination isn't occurring. When using a selection procedure, ask yourself if there is a fairer way to do it that still accomplishes your business needs and your need to protect the public. And having done that, that's about as safe as you can play it. You still may go to court, but you'll be better off if you've followed the guidelines above.

STUDY QUESTIONS

- You select John Doe for a job. John gets drunk on the job, gets in a company vehicle, and has a wreck with another driver. Is John's behavior your responsibility?
- Does EEOC validate tests?
- Is it true that an employer may not use a test that discriminates against a racial group?
- Do you have any legal liability after you hire people?
- Company Acme Business hires about 30% of white applicants and 26% of their black applicants. The Human Resources Director maintains her "numbers are good." Are they?

CHAPTER 9

THE INTERVIEW AND OTHER ALTERNATIVES TO TESTING

- The interview is a test, and generally a bad one!
- The interview has many flaws that are not present in standardized tests.
- Properly done, the interview does have its place.
- Why not use all of our tools, including testing, interviewing, and everything else?

Why is radiation treatment used for cancer? It isn't always effective. It often has side effects. The answer, obviously, is that in some cases it is the best alternative. Thus, we have a flawed system of justice, education, and so forth, because no one has developed anything better.

Surprisingly, many people criticize testing but fail to mention a better *alternative*. Their actions and criticisms imply that if testing is not used, results will be much better, but they do not specify nor even hint at what that "perfect alternative" might be. And since it is not possible to "do nothing" you must have some alternative.

Let's take as a given that there is no *perfect* alternative. Is the frequently mentioned interview a *better* alternative? If not, why is it so commonly held up as a option? Let's look hard at the interview.

The Interview

If you, your client, your company, or anyone you know is planning to rely on the interview for selection, please have them read this chapter and the chapter notes at the end of the book. Blind use of the interview can be a serious blunder.

A strange story will set the stage for our discussion. A story about people who advocate dropping the use of an imperfect tool in order to replace it with one that is far less effective and proven to be more discriminatory.

A Strange Story

Business owners are concerned with honesty and drug usage, as well they should be. Theft and the use of drugs on the job cost businesses a great deal, a cost which in large part is passed on to the consumer. People who use drugs can cause harm to other people. Yes, business owners are concerned with the concept of integrity. What will they use to gauge these critical traits?

Integrity tests are a subset of personality tests that have many problems. The use of integrity tests has been criticized and even banned in Massachusetts. Critics of integrity tests point out that the tests are often invasive, far from perfect, and have the potential for "false positives," that is, branding someone as dishonest who is not. These comments are all *true*, but what is strange is the number of people who see the interview as an alternative!

Yes, integrity tests are far from perfect, but most have some evidence to support their validity. The interview is not only imperfect, it operates at chance level in the detection of truth telling. Some integrity tests ask unnecessarily invasive items, but the interview is frequently a place where off-the-wall questions occur. Integrity test data show no discrimination by race or gender while the interview is greatly affected by stereotypes and frequently discriminates against women.

Strange indeed, to take a flawed tool and argue for replacing it with an even more flawed tool. Would anyone argue that a drug with side effects be replaced with a drug known to have more and worse side effects? Yet, this very argument is made with regard to the interview. Read on to learn why this happens.

Why is the Interview So Commonly Used?

There are good and bad reasons. The good reason is that there is some information exchanged in an interview that cannot be exchanged in a testing situation. That's not a reason to drop the usage of tests, but it is a reason to use the interview, as we will discuss later. Let's look at the unfortunately *bad* reasons that most people use the interview in selection and the equally *bad* reasons that many job candidates want to be interviewed.

Some job applicants feel stymied by a cold and impersonal test instrument. They imagine they could talk their way into a job if only they could deal with another flesh-and-blood person. They feel that, at last, someone will give them a thorough hearing.

In fact, interviewers are more likely to be discriminatory than tests. They look at the wrong things and jump to conclusions. They often have their minds made up 5 minutes into the interview. And, if they have an application blank or other data, they may have their minds made up before the interview even begins.

Most interviewers consider themselves excellent judges of people. They put a great deal of trust in their ability to read body language, facial expressions, subtle cues in speech, and so forth.

In fact, most people—even those with expert credentials—cannot read other people with nearly the accuracy they imagine. They have a confidence in their abilities that is simply not warranted.

Many employers feel that people might be insulted by tests, giving a bad reputation to the company, while interviewers will present a favorable image.

In fact, litigation has often been triggered because interviewers were not respectful and said things that are inappropriate and even offensive.

Some people use the interview because it seems safe, free from the legal hassles associated with testing. Human Resources Directors attend half-day seminars and tell their management not to use the litigious test.

In fact, the interview is a test in every legal sense. And it is a poor test at that.

Many decision makers simply have false information and/or assumptions they haven't bothered to examine. Let's debunk the hallowed interview once and for all. Once again, with feeling, no standardized test is perfect; but since the interview is even *further* from perfection, we will use it for a contrast.

Facts About the Interview

The interview is a test

Read the Uniform Guidelines. Look at court cases (a small sample is given in the chapter notes). The interview is not *sui generis*, not an selection instrument in a class all its own—it is a *test*, just as much as any paper and pencil instrument. In addition, it is a remarkably poor test as we will show below.

Interviewers jump to conclusions

A 40-item test is going to be evaluated based on all 40 items. In a 15-minute interview, most interviewers make up their minds in the first 4 minutes.

Interviewers dwell on negatives

In a 40-item test, the right answers are evaluated as well as the wrong answers. Interviewers tend to place more emphasis on negative information.

Interviewers look at the wrong things

One can argue that test users may use test measurements, for example, ego strength, in job situations where that trait is not relevant. That is a common fault of the interview. Interviewers often look at irrelevant cues in making evaluations. The interviewee may think he/she is doing a good job of presenting his/her qualifications while the interviewer notices that his/her legs are crossed and draws deep conclusions based on that "body language" data.

Interviewers let stereotypes affect their judgment

Face it, an objectively scored test is going to be scored the same way for men and women, young and old, black or white. Interviewers, being human, have stereotypes about people. You and I and members of *our* group (whatever that group may be) tend to be evaluated as individuals. They and them and members of that *other* group (whatever that group may be) tend to be viewed in terms of stereotypes.

It's encouraging to note that racial stereotypes are declining across the years—nevertheless, they still remain. White people are bigots, black people are lazy, orientals are detail oriented, Germans are tidy but cruel...and so forth.

Do interviewers let these stereotypes affect them? Of course. Women, in particular, regardless of behavior, are evaluated differently than men by both male and female interviewers. And this is unfortunate, since the skills to succeed in some jobs (e.g., management) are the same!

Interviewers are subjective and inconsistent

Some tests such as cognitive tests have only one interpretation. Other tests, such as personality tests, may be used in a formulized actuarial manner or may be interpreted in a clinical manner. The clinical interpretation involves some subjectivity. But even at its most subjective, test interpretation is based on *some* guidelines. The interview is often conducted without any guidelines.

An objective test has the same questions, asked the same way, scored the same way, in each testing situation. Unless it is carefully structured, interviews tend to vary from person to person and from case to case with the same interviewer.

When job interviews are challenged in court (which they often are) the court looks at consistency and job relevance. And the consistency factor is one that most interviews simply do not have. This inconsistency necessarily keeps job relevance low (how can it be relevant if it's different every time?) As the court said of the interview process in *United States v. Hazelwood School District* (1976), "No evidence was presented which would indicate that any two principals apply the same criteria—objective or subjective—to evaluate applicants."

Do you know what your interviewers are telling people?

You know exactly what the test is asking and saying. Do you know that for your (many) interviewers in a typical company?

The interview is usually a bad test

The interview is a test that can be challenged and frequently has been challenged and has been found wanting. That's hardly surprising.

Interviews tend to be conducted in an unsystematic manner by human beings who, being human, tend to let stereotypes affect their perception particularly of people who are not part of their group. They evaluate the same traits in women differently than in men. They vary their questions from case to case and they reach different conclusions based on the same data. They often make snap judgments. They tend to dwell on negatives rather than positives and they often scrutinize irrelevant details instead of listening to what is being said. Interviewers are not monitored in most cases, so the company cannot be sure what is being said by the interviewer—and what is said can have terribly negative results. Standardized tests are far from perfect, but they commit none of those errors.

Yes, the interview *can* be done better and it can have value, as we will discuss in the next section. But, by and large, interviews are done in the unskilled and unstructured manner that leads to nothing more or less than a bad test.

The interview does have a place!

Despite everything that has been said, the interview does have a place, an important place, in the employment process. It will be used.

If interviews are structured to be consistently conducted and evaluated, they can be valid. In other words, to the extent that interviews are like standardized tests, they are effective.

But the interview has strengths that are the flip side of its negatives. It is not consistent, it is flexible—the interviewer who hears an off-hand derogatory statement about women can pursue that issue. The interviewer who notices that the interviewee is close to tears may find that this person has had a recent loss and may determine that testing and interviewing is inappropriate at that time.

It is subjective, and subjectivity can be valuable. The interviewer who has a bad "gut feel" can ask questions to see if there are problems or if he is simply having heartburn.

It is not formulized. Only human judgment can integrate information in those many situations where no formula exists. In short, there are many functions of the interview that an impersonal test cannot provide.

People *are* going to interview. Whether or not it is accurate, we all feel the need to see people face to face before we hire them. Let's consider some guidelines for making the interview more effective. There are some common-sense but often overlooked essentials, including:

- Always be tactful and polite. Never call a woman a "girl" and don't use cute names.

- Don't say anything stupid. It will get your company sued.

- Remember that the interviewer should do 25% or less of the talking.

- Regardless of any "pop psych" you may have read do *not* put anyone under stress.

- Ask "yes/no" questions (e.g., "Did you like your last job") sparingly and depend on "open end" questions (e.g., "Tell me about your last job").

- Don't overestimate your ability. Depend on what the candidate tells you, not on your ability to read body language. At *most*, use body language as a source of hypothesis to be tested with questions.

- Demand examples. ("Frank, you say you're creative. Can you give me an example of something creative you've done?")

- Look for trends, for example, never gets along with superiors, always enjoys a fast pace, changes jobs frequently.

- Look for gaps in employment dates and qualified statements ("Yes, I got along with almost everyone").

- Make sure your question is answered

    Interviewer: "Can you tell me why you left your last job?"

    Interviewee: "I felt it was time for a change."

  Note: The question was not answered.

- Go back and ask a question again. If it isn't answered, wait, rephrase it, and ask it again later ("Tom, earlier you said that you felt it was time for a change. Why was it time for a change?")

- Don't make up your mind in the first 5 minutes.

- Listen to all information, not just the negatives.

- Remember that a person can be good in one area and poor in another. Don't fall into the "halo effect" of rating people all good or all bad.

- Close the interview with thanks and a handshake and let the candidate know when you will contact him/her again.

That's not enough for a good interview, but it's a good start. There are books (e.g., *The Employer's Guide to Interviewing*, Genua, 1979) on interviewing. Read several and pick out the best points.

Some people may advocate rescuing the interview by structuring it. But, if you're going to make the interview standardized in terms of questions and evaluations, why not take one step further and make it a test? And, if you're going to evaluate things like sociability or work interest why not use the existing instruments that have been studied and evaluated for years?

As an addition to testing, the interview is very valuable to picking up those crucial bits of information that standardized testing cannot. For management and executive jobs there may be many job-fit factors that a general test will not sufficiently address. An addition, yes, but the interview is not, and should not be, a substitute for testing. At worst it is a subjective tool that may be, as the court described unstructured performance reviews "...a ready mechanism for discrimination..." At best it is a pseudo-test that will be a poor second choice.

Other Alternatives to Testing

Assessment Centers

In an *assessment center,* people spend a day or so performing simulated work activities while being observed and graded by raters. The ratings of assessment centers are often quite valid and reliable. The problem with an assessment center is the cost involved. Imagine having to fill every position by having every applicant spend a day of time or even several hours being observed by trained raters.

For management, executive, sales, and professional positions, assessment centers may be warranted. These need not be an alternative to testing but can be used in conjunction with testing. Testing improves the validity of the assessment center.

Evaluation of Experience

Instead of using a testing, interviewing, or assessment center why not just check experience and/or education requirements?

Good idea to a certain point. But, remember, experience and education requirements are tests, tests that have been tried in the courts and found wanting in some cases. The difficulty with experience is defining what, for example, "2 years of experience in computers" means. Does that mean operating a computer, writing a program or using canned programs? Also, it may look job related, but how can you prove it? Why should a person with 2 years of experience be given preference over someone with 1 1/2? While it may seem obvious to you that education is a predictor of success, it may not be universally accepted by other people. Even if the job demands literacy, it may not demand *education* (see the chapter notes).

If you're going to include education and experience in your selection procedure, have some rationale for why you're doing it—don't do it just because it's easy. Be specific about experience, including whether the person assisted in the work, did the work without supervision, or supervised other people who were doing it. Once again, experience and education can (and should) be used in conjunction with testing. Read about biodata in chapter 6.

Reference Checks

If you look at reference checks as a stand-alone test, they don't work well. They have questionable validity, and how could they be consistent? Many organizations refuse, as a matter of policy, to give out information about previous employees. Reference checks *should* be conducted because of the possibility of the rare occurrence of finding that someone has simply falsified information about previous jobs held. In addition, while most companies have a policy against giving any reference information, if you ask nicely, someone will usually talk to you. Again, it is *not* a substitute for testing.

A Final Thought: Why Not Use All Our Tools?

Why should any tool be an alternative? Why not use testing, interviewing, experience, and education requirements, assessment centers, and any other tools to help you make a decision? Use each one for the selection component that it does best.

STUDY QUESTIONS

- Interviewers with several years of experience can generally detect lying, true or false?
- Education requirements are tests that have been tried in court, true or false?

CHAPTER 10

ISSUES OF FREQUENT CONCERN

- Some concerns about testing are simply misplaced. Tests are not anti-employee, and they are better than any evaluation alternative.
- Some concerns about testing have to be addressed, and they can be.

To be tested means to be evaluated, categorized, and perhaps found wanting. Not surprisingly, there are some concerns and some gripes that you as a test user will encounter.

Misplaced Concerns

"Misplaced" because, while the parties complaining have good intentions, they misunderstand or misperceive the situation.

Minorities never do well on tests

First, let's break the question down into the *type* of test. If you're talking about interest, personality, or integrity, minorities do as well as the white majority. On cognitive tests, whites as a *group* do tend to do better than blacks as a *group*. We will address this serious issue below. But don't lump every standardized instrument into the same "test" package when talking about differential performance.

Testing is not as valid, reliable, fair, consistent, and so forth as it should be!

Gently, because it's no good offending people, gently rephrase the statement so that it makes sense...by adding: "compared to what?"

The ladder is not as long as it should be! Do you have one that's longer? The justice system is not perfect! Do you know a system that is better? People—even educated people—fall into the trap of the "perfect alternative."

No, tests are not perfectly valid—what is? Yes, people can discriminate against using tests—they can discriminate using tests, interviews, application blanks, handwriting...

Most legal hassles involve hiring!

People who would never think of using an unvalidated test, people who scrutinize the interview carefully, will quickly promote Joe because he has a better attitude than Mary. The underlying assumption is that hiring is the only area that involves liability. In *Rowe v. General Motors* (1972) it was *promotion* that was questioned. In 1990, less than 9% of EEOC claims were about hiring—over 60% were about advancement or discharge (Lublin, 1991)! (Read chapter 8.)

Tests are flawed and legally liable! The interview is the better choice!

Yes, odd though it may seem, some people make that argument. Read chapter 9 to find out just *how* flawed that argument is.

Tests are flawed and legally liable! It's best to use the better hiring tools that are available!

What are those tools? Reference checks, interviews, application blanks are certainly not as good, much less better! They are often proposed, nevertheless.

Business is dumb and anti-employee!

This isn't specifically test related, but it underlies many concerns in all aspects of hiring, promoting, firing, and retiring. The idea of a big, monolithic, impersonal machine that grinds people up and spits them out for unknown and impractical reasons is a very common one.

Most business is, in fact, more along the lines of Mom and Pop than IBM. And businesses, large and small, are aware of the fact that business functions best when people are treated correctly. It is NOT the goal of most businesses to hurt people. Business leaders are surprisingly intelligent people who realize (and realized long before psychologists "proved" it) that people who are hardworking and smart tend to do better jobs than people who are not and that people who are willing to deal with people in a persuasive manner are more successful as managers and salesmen than those who are not. Business leaders understand the concept of saving a dollar using a flawed device as opposed losing one by using an even *more* flawed device. Business leaders know that putting someone in a job for which he/she is not suited is not doing a favor to the individual. Testing, interviewing, and reference checking is not done because the executives on the top floor have a prurient interest in gazing at personality test scores. It is, rather, because hiring mistakes can be extremely costly and can even destroy a business.

Tests keep people from getting jobs!

This is an unjustified but common concern. In most cases, employers make a decision about the number of people they are going to hire for a given job. Let's say the number is 10. If employers don't use testing they will probably hire 10 people. If they do use testing, they will probably hire—10 people. The only difference is that the use of testing will probably result in a better selection of 10 people for their purposes. In addition, the 10 people who get the job with the assistance of testing will probably be the ones who most deserved and will most *enjoy* the job.

Tests don't work!

This concern is seldom mentioned in light of present-day research. At one time there was a feeling that cognitive tests were simply vehicles for culturally biased and unfair discrimination, with no real relationship to work. There is now a wealth of information showing that cognitive tests can predict performance in practically every type of job. For centuries, the great civilizations of Europe, Africa, Asia, and the Americas emphasized the importance of reading, writing, logic, and math. Is it any surprise that such abilities are related to work success? We taught the 3 Rs for a reason!

Personality tests were once held in disdain, even by psychologists, despite business wisdom that said personal traits were of paramount importance in business. Once again, research has finally caught up with common sense. For some positions, personality tests are extremely useful in predicting future performance. Success in managerial occupations, for example, can be predicted decades in advance through testing.

Bottom line—good tests give very good information. Even when the relationship between the test and the success measure appears small it can be extremely useful. See the notes for chapter 2, which discuss "variance accounted for."

Employers are dropping the use of testing!

This is a common claim, but nothing more than wishful thinking on the part of people who are antitest. Business leaders are very intelligent, and they know that testing works. In a 1992 survey, only 10% of Human Resource executives anticipated a drop in testing (due to economic reasons), 60% expected it to stay the same, and 30% expected an increase.

Honesty testing is unreasonable!

There is a class of tests known as honesty or integrity tests, which attempt to determine integrity, usually in the very concrete form of theft and drug usage. Some of these tests have been challenged as being invasive and unreasonable, and some no doubt are. Some states have outlawed honesty tests. On the other hand, making an attempt to determine honesty is hardly unreasonable.

Business loses $40 billion per year due to employee theft. Drugs are a major problem in productivity.

And this is not merely a problem for fat cats in the executive boardroom. Consumers must pay this cost. Of every dollar you pay for your steaks, sweaters, and books, as much as 15¢ pays for employee theft.

It is not surprising that businesses are eager to do anything possible to combat losses due to theft and employee misconduct. Ernst and Young's *Survey of Retail Loss Prevention* (1992) found that almost half of the businesses were using honesty testing and more intended to do so.

Given the potential for loss of profit, it is quite reasonable to employers to want to know which employees are most likely to be honest—and the alternative to honesty testing is what? Gut feel in the interview?

If you're not sure of which side of the honesty test debate you're on, read the chapter notes.

Honesty tests that are based on unnecessary invasion, "have you stopped beating your wife" questions and broad inferences based on scant data are unreasonable, no doubt. But don't throw out the entire idea without examining the specific test. And don't throw out the honesty test and use an alternative that's even worse—such as an interview! Read the "strange story" portion of chapter 9 for a comparison of honesty tests with the interview.

Tests have high false positives!

In this case, a false positive refers to, for example, labeling someone as "dishonest" when they are, in fact, honest. In the first place, there is nothing unique about tests in generating false positives. In addition, the acceptable level for false positive depends on the gravity of the situation.

Critics can and will play with statistics, especially when large numbers and low probabilities are involved. A recent popular press article pointed out that a drug test that was 95% accurate could lead to implicating as many nondrug users as drug users. In the first place, many drug tests are more than 95% accurate. But, many tests are not, so let's use 95% accurate as an example.

Odd though that sounds, if only 5% of the population are drug users and the test is 95% accurate, you can use statistics to gain the result of implicating as many non-drug users as drug users with a drug screen. Sounds like a fifty-fifty, but the following is also undeniably true: Given that you are not a drug user, your probability of being identified as a drug user is not fifty-fifty, it's .05. And here's another way of looking at the situation.

Suppose Airline A uses that "coin flip" drug test for their pilots. It is 95% accurate, and only 5% of the population uses drugs. Of their 1,000 pilots, less than 3 are drug users. Airline B *doesn't* use that test, and 50 of the pilots (only about 18 times more) use drugs. Airline C has bravely decided to hire the pilots who failed the invasive drug test (someone said something about fifty-fifty, why that's just a coin flip) and of their 1,000 pilots *500* use drugs. You're about to buy a ticket for your 9-year old daughter...which airline do you want? Think hard.

If you ever face this type of fifty-fifty reasoning (and you will) use the Airline Story.

It's fifty-fifty, so it's chance level

Most people think of chance as a coin flip, and anyone knows that the probability of getting a head is .50 and the probability of getting a tail is .50. That's because there are only two alternatives! In many cases a .50 probability has nothing to do with chance. For example, if you get a royal flush 10 hands out of 20, that's fifty-fifty, but it's not chance level—friend, you're cheating.

You've never actually shown

Of all of the concerns that are expressed, one that may surprise you is the attorney or critic who asks, "Mr. Smith, have you ever actually shown that this test of reading ability has any relationship to the job of copy editor?"

"No," you stammer, "but it seems..."

"Aha! You haven't shown that this test predicts this job success!"

It is rare in any area of life, including the physical sciences to demonstrate the truth of every proposition. You haven't actually shown that getting hit by a 1989 Oldsmobile going 62 miles per hour would hurt you, but assume it would! Scientists had never actually been to Jupiter nor seen anything other than a bright circle at one time, but they knew its size and shape to a level of accuracy later verified by actual observation of space probes.

In almost all areas of life we have to use a logical web of evidence; we have "actually shown" practically none of the things we accept as true in our lives.

The government needs to protect people from tests!

The law can and does govern the use of testing—and other selection devices—so it will be done in a fair manner. Where the law specifically attempts to control one *type* of device rather than the *manner* in which it is used, it inevitably takes always someone's rights! Read the chapter notes for one bizarre example.

Of course you say that, you're biased

Some testing critics simply don't have the right information. Others don't want to hear the information, and a convenient way to dismiss it is by pointing out that the research has been done with a bias. One attorney criticizes pro-test opinions "...especially the conclusions and opinions of persons who earn their professional livelihood in the field in question" (Seymour, 1988).

Good point. But, like the perfect alternative, who is the unbiased expert? Some psychologists derive income from testing and have a bias toward proving that tests work. Some attorneys make their living by successfully winning cases against testing, whether that success is based on fact or not; one might expect they would have a bias toward seeing the flaws in testing. Some people want job representation on the basis of quota rather than qualification; they might have a bias against objective measures if they feel their group is likely to fall short.

Some union leaders have a bias toward pleasing their membership rather than finding psychometric validity. Some business leaders have a bias toward getting the best people whether or not that means insuring equal representation for all groups. Some politicians have a bias toward getting re-elected rather than finding the best selection tools. In fact, who *can* prove that he/she is totally unbiased?

It is a serious logical error (called the *fallacy of origin*) to condemn an argument solely based on whether one likes the author of the argument. Let's assume we are all human and have some biases. Then let's work toward what is best for all concerned, individual job candidates, employers who drive our economy, and the public affected by the quality of people who serve them.

You're wrong, so I'm right

In the area of employment, you can line up people on various sides, each claiming that finding flaws in the "other side's" argument supports their own. This creates a great deal of heat with no light.

Logically, two ideas are *contradictory* if the invalidation of one supports the truth of the other (if you can prove the number is not odd, it must be even); two ideas are *contrary* if both could be false, but they can't both be true (it can't be solid white *and* solid black; it could be solid green). Most ideas in testing are not contradictory, nor even contrary.

We must realize that tests can be seriously flawed *and* be the best alternative for selection, that tests may be valid predictors of some types of job success *and* discriminate against some groups, and that the interview may be essential *and* be inappropriate as a sole selection device. Let's focus on finding the best alternatives, even if that involves compromise. Follow the advice of Fisher and Ury (1981) and focus on underlying *concerns* rather than stated *positions*. For example, in the case of cognitive test use, consider the suggestions in chapter 11.

Concerns That Have Some Basis

Some concerns have some basis, unlike the card-trick "coin flip drug test" or the people who fret about tests without reading the Uniform Guidelines (and court cases), which clearly identify all selection procedures as tests.

Tests discriminate unfairly against minorities!

Any selection device could discriminate against a group, and that discrimination might be fair—that is, job related—or unfair.

Personality tests *aren't* likely to have a discriminatory effect. In sales, extraversion is an important factor, but there's no reason to expect to find fewer extraverted blacks than whites or women than men. In fact, some research shows that blacks are relatively more likely than whites to have interest in business and sales rather than technical interests; and business and sales are associated with success in business. In some cases black candidates score lower than whites on cognitive measures but compensate with greater interpersonal skills. As we have seen in the section on the interview, successful female and male managers have similar traits.

But we mustn't be glib in talking about *cognitive* tests. This is a sensitive area, and cognitive tests are now and are likely to be, controversial for the following reasons:

1. Unlike personality tests in which a number of combinations might be possible with no single "right" way to be, there is a single "right" way to score on cognitive tests—high.

2. Many scholars argue convincingly that cognitive ability is related to performance on practically every job. And indeed, what jobs do not require intelligence?

3. As a group, blacks score lower on cognitive tests. The use of cognitive tests as a hurdle will almost certainly lead to adverse impact if applied to the general population of blacks and whites. Why?

Decades ago, some researchers showed differences in IQ and reasoned from this that blacks were genetically inferior—despite some obvious flaws in that reasoning. Another camp started with the premise that there certainly were no differences between the races and that traditional tests contained culture-biased items. The culture-biased group claimed tests that gauged "intelligence" were assessing the common knowledge of the *white* culture. Sure, white kids might more readily recognize George Washington but would they know George Washington Carver? The average white man might be likely to know the capital of France, but would he know what was on the bottom of "boxcars?" Thus, the search was on for a *culture fair* test.

After many years, the results are clear. Research findings show that "culture fair" tests discriminate *against* blacks. Cognitive tests, whether "culturally biased" or "culture fair" *did* predict job performance. The search failed.

Of course it failed! Does anyone wonder why African-Americans like Dr. King were willing to die in the fight for equality, especially equality in education? In 1960 Dr. King heralded "...a steady decline in crippling illiteracy." He spoke of the "...evil system of segregation." Why would he be so concerned about education? If the "3 Rs" were no more important than rolling dice, why all the fuss? If education has no practical effect on knowledge why ask that it be improved? Clearly, he *did* feel education is important. And education is directly seen in cognitive tests.

If someone with a deficient diet is given a physical exam and found to be less healthy, are you going to blame the physical exam? Should you "doctor" the exam to hide the effects of a deficient diet? What nonsense!

If someone with a second-class education is given a cognitive test and found to be less astute, are you going to blame the test? Should you "doctor" the exam to hide the effects of that inadequate education? What nonsense!

Unless you make the Polyanna assumption that the civil rights war was won in the 1960s, there are many African-Americans in the work force who had second-class educations in the public schools. As a society we can't bury our heads and say, "it never happened, and even if it did it didn't have an impact." Discrimination arguably *is*, but definitely *was,* a fact, and its impact continues.

Don't assume cognitive tests will be unfair in *all* cases. In some cases the preselection "washes out" effects of race. In one search for legal counsel I tested a number of people including some blacks. The blacks scored as high or higher than their white peers. Such a select sample of people go to law school, much less finish, much less have the attainments necessary for legal counsel that any effects of race long since washed out, by the time I saw and tested the final candidates.

Still, we are left with the problem that exists for the larger population of blacks and whites. How are we going to break the cycle of excluding people for problems not of their making? In the final chapter of this book I make some suggestions.

It's easy to fake personality tests

Personality tests, especially those that are self-report, can be faked. You can answer questions differently than you are. But there are some other pertinent pieces of information:

- While people can fake, they usually don't.
- You have to be reasonably well adjusted and confident in order to know the "correct" answers.
- "Fake scales" are always correlated with emotional health.

In summary: People with social and emotional problems have a hard time faking a positive personality profile, some people can fake but they usually don't. Not surprisingly, personality tests can predict success in a wide range of areas as much as 20 years in the future.

Tests are invasive!

This is potentially very serious in a society that places high value on individual freedom. Honesty or integrity tests, as discussed above, are often assailed, and one of the main reasons is the type of questions asked (see comments by Attorney Seligman in BNA's *Employee Relations Weekly*, June 11, 1990; see discussion of *Soroka* in chapter notes.)

Invasion is a critical issue. Let's define *invasive*. What about this: requested information, especially of a personal nature, is invasive if it does not have direct application to the job. A test that asks about your drinking habits is invasive. A test that asks about your drinking at work is much less invasive. If you're going to fly a commercial aircraft, a test that asks about your drinking at work is anything but invasive!

The key is to look at test items, information that can be seen by the employer, information that might leak out to other people, and the importance of the test item to the trait being measured relative to the position. If the information bears on something that can affect profitability, it is the employer's business. If it affects human life, (whatever it is) it is *not* invasive. If very personal information is being examined for prurient or just careless reasons, it is invasive.

Tests pigeonhole people

Again, let's not go overboard against tests; written interviewer comments can pigeonhole people just as effectively as any test score. In addition (see section and chapter notes on "tests don't work"), people do not show major changes in intellect or personality in the normal course of events. Having said that, this is also true: We should never forget that test scores are static and people are dynamic. People can learn, overcome person limitations, and they can better themselves. It's like losing weight: Most people won't, anybody can, a few people do.

CHAPTER 11

FUTURE OF TESTING

- Prediction: Test use will continue to grow and improve.
- Prediction: Evaluation of validity will continue to focus on an appraisal of the best available alternative.
- Suggestion: Hiring is fine, but let's use tests more extensively for personal development!

Someday a hologram test administrator will be able to be accessed at any time or place to quickly administer tests orally in the language of the participant's choice. That's a dream, of course, but it may come to pass before we know it.

Predictions

1. In the immediate future, testing will continue to improve as data banks grow on existing tests and research into cognition and personality improves our understanding of those two areas.

2. We will see continuing debate concerning the 1991 Civil Rights Act outlining of separate cut scores (see Adler, 1993).

3. Computerized testing will continue to grow along with other new test-delivery technologies, for example, video testing, telephone testing, publicly available terminals, and these technologies will reduce the distortion areas.

4. Concern will continue to focus on being respectful and noninvasive while gathering needed information. Strange-sounding and invasive test items won't weather criticism by a purely empirical argument.

5. The new and powerful Item Response Theory will continue to be developed. By focusing on the relationship of individual items to overall prediction, tests can be shortened to fit the individual needs (e.g., if an individual can answer a hard question, why not "shortcut" and avoid giving her the easier ones; if he can't answer an easy question, why waste his time giving him harder items?). Related prediction: it will take longer than many people will like because: (1) the research requires large numbers of subjects and (2) in practice, it will be hard to prove that two people are testing fairly when they take a quite different test.

6. Courts will follow the trend of thinking of the psychological community and emphasize solid logical reasoning as opposed to so-called empirical validity.

Suggestions

1. Let's use tests even more aggressively in the area of personal development and training diagnostics. Even if you knew exactly who you wanted to hire, testing them can still be an invaluable tool. Who needs assertiveness training? Who needs to brush up on basic math? Who fits best in different roles?

2. *Let's face the cognitive testing ability head on and recognize that it is a cognitive ability issue.* Of course, tests of reading, writing, and arithmetic show a superiority for whites; it's the result of years of discrimination, which civil rights heroes fought (and fight) against so bravely. Of course, reading, writing, and arithmetic predict job performance; why else would we (and every other civilization throughout the world) place such an emphasis on it?

   We have seen many people argue that cognitive tests predict job success and therefore should be used. Other people complain that cognitive tests discriminate against blacks and therefore should not be used. Please note: the opposition lies in the result of highest priority, not the underlying argument. In point of fact, cognitive tests discriminate against blacks as a group and successfully predict work performance in many jobs. What's the way out? Let me suggest:

   - Use cognitive tests with reasonable cut scores, no higher than necessary to do the job.

   - Use cognitive tests that are specific (vocabulary and math) rather than general.

   - Use tests for *diagnostic* purposes rather than elimination from consideration. For example, give that math test and then use the scores to focus at-work training programs in math.

   - Use cognitive tests in conjunction with other measures, especially personality measures. In sales, for example, if you were given a choice between an extrovert with a moderate IQ and an introvert with an extremely high IQ, your choice would be obvious—go with the outgoing person. Intelligence may be important in any job, but sometimes it is not the most important factor.

3. Let's use personality and integrity tests—which are unlikely to discriminate by race or gender—and, in specific, those personality and integrity tests that come no closer to invasiveness than *demanded* by the job. Personality factors such as sociability are very important—vital—in jobs such as sales and management. But let's not demand that every software engineer be extremely outgoing. Don't ask someone about drinking habits if there is no likelihood that drinking on the job would occur or have an effect if it did.

4. Recognize the duty we all have to the public as well as the employee. No one wants to see a person denied a job or embarrassed by invasive questions. No one wants to see an oil spill due to a drunk captain nor people at work hurt by a deranged co-worker, either!

5. Any time a debate focuses on the limitations of tests, refocus the debate on finding the best alternatives. It's easy to criticize practically any system; it's not so easy to come up with a better alternative, including "doing nothing."

SELF-TESTS

Think you know your way around testing? Take the following self-test. Score yourself and then re-read sections for any items you miss.

Self-Test 1

1. A test, by EEOC standards, refers to any paper and pencil device that is scored and used to make an employment decision.

2. The WAIS is a popular personality inventory.

3. A test item "I like brown dogs" is consistently related to success in mechanical drawing, even though we have no idea why—we're using this test item based on an empirical approach.

4. Reliability refers to the stability of test results for an individual over time.

5. Biodata refers to attitudes toward life in general.

6. By increasing your "hit" rate you can decrease the false positive rate to zero.

7. A culture fair test that is nonverbal will practically never discriminate among races.

8. Statistical significance refers to the percentage of time you will make correct decisions using a test, for example, if the test is significant at the .05 level, you will be correct 95 out of a 100 times.

9. In order to select XR9-language computer programmers you give them a test that consists of questions relating to the XR9 language. You make no claims about underlying theory, and you have no success data relative to the test. You merely claim that the test covers the same information that programmers will actually deal with. You say your test is content valid.

10. In order to select machine operators, you give them a test that contains various colors that they are to match according to their preferences. You have no data to suggest that this color matching is related to machine operation skill and the job itself will not involve colors. Nevertheless, the Neo-Freudian theory of color matching says individuals who prefer red are very perceptive, and your work environment demands perceptiveness. You claim your test is criterion valid.

11. You have one test that measures speed of learning and another that measures persistence. Your research has shown that one ability can compensate for the other. For example, a person who learns slowly but is persistent is often as good as a person who learns more quickly but is not as persistent. You correctly elect NOT to use a multiple cutoff method of test use.

12. A correlation of .30 between measure 1 and measure 2 means that if you use measure 1 (a test, for example), it will correctly predict measure 2 (some measure of success, for example) in 30% of the cases.

13. I am creating a test of judgment. I examine each item to see if it sounds like it measures good judgment based on my expert analysis of the factors involved. I am using a factor-analytic approach to test development.

14. You select John Doe for a job. John gets drunk on the job, gets in a company vehicle, and has a wreck with another driver. Your company can be responsible for negligent hiring.

15. The five factors most commonly identified in the assessment of personality are: sociability, neuroticism, humor, openness to new ideas, and nervousness.

16. If the reliability of a test is .64, the validity can be no higher than .80.

17. If the reliability of a test is .64, the validity could be .20.

18. It is important to use only those tests that are validated by the EEOC.

19. If you use a test in an employment setting, it must be validated for EEOC purposes.

20. An employer may not use a test that discriminates against a racial group.

21. If adverse impact is shown, the employer must show the validity of his selection procedure as a whole.

22. If a score of 19 is higher than 85% of the scores in that norm group, it is said to be at the 85th percentile.

23. A test that measures ability to reason with stated problems is a cognitive test.

24. John scores 6 out of 20 correct, (no correction for guessing), a score that is at the 55th percentile by male college student norms. His raw score is 55.

25. I have scores for 10 college women: 42,45,46,50,50,50,51,51,52,60. The mode is 50.

26. A clinical approach is always more accurate than a mere statistical or actuarial approach.

27. While people can fake personality tests, this is usually not a problem for predictability.

28. The interview has been found to be an "invalid test" in some cases.

29. The Strong Campbell Interest Inventory is a measure of vocational interests.

30. No one can be totally assured that his company won't be sued for using or not using a selection procedure.

31. Businesses would have more employees if it weren't for testing.

32. Biodata will not discriminate against any group.

33. Courts don't have to go by the guidelines in ruling on a case.

34. An employer can avoid EEOC test scrutiny by not using tests—sometimes the best idea.

35. Frank does a test to see if blacks score lower than whites. He looks at the scores for 10 black applicants and 10 white applicants and finds no significant difference. However, as Bill correctly points out, the groups may still be different even though the statistic came out nonsignificant.

36. Dr. Jack Expert wants you to use the XYZ Math Test in hiring for all your hourly people. He tells you not to worry—the test is valid. Is his assertion true or false?

37. If you have a test that successfully predicts supervisory ratings, it is valid by EEOC standards and practical business standards.

38. With hard criterion such as sales volume for salesmen, the criterion is obviously a good one because there is no subjectivity in its measurement and nothing but performance that can influence it.

39. It's best to have a test as long as possible, because the longer the test the greater the reliability and validity.

40. The job of secretary at Somestore, Inc., involves the following important components: 20% typing, 10% filing, 10% answering the phone, 40% greeting clients, and 20% scheduling. They use a typing test to make the hiring decision. Since it is content valid, it meets EEOC requirements if it is ever challenged.

41. Asking personal questions that have little or no bearing on the job is invasive.

42. Years of research show that the job of policeman demands someone who can handle stress. I have a stress test with years of supporting evidence. But when I tested 15 policemen rated "highly effective" against 15 policemen rated "highly ineffective" good performance correlated *negatively* with stress coping and it was significant at the .05 level! I'm not going to use the test to pick low scorers, however, because the result doesn't make sense. Good decision, true or false?

43. You have just taken over the Human Resources Manager position. You don't want to make unnecessary changes in the selection program but you question one aspect of the selection procedure—people are given preference for the warehouse jobs if they score high on a "sports knowledge" test. You protest that this is leading to the hiring of fewer women than men. The warehouse foreman shows you a rather impressive validity study showing that people who score high in sports interests also load and unload the shelves faster. You find it hard to argue with the hard data, but you *still* feel that the test is likely to be unfair.

44. You are helping Gadget, Inc., a start-up company, hire salespeople. You know and Gadget knows that good salespeople are smart. The sharp-looking guys and gals you interview are all high scorers on your cognitive test. You

do a validation study using a good cognitive test with sales volume as one criterion and the salesperson's personal satisfaction as the other. You want people who can sell a lot and enjoy their job. The 200 salespeople in the field have been on board about an equal time, and no one has an unusually easy or unusually hard area. You have a wide spread of intelligence scores and criteria scores. The intelligence test correlates .09—nonsignificant— with sales volume. And it correlates significantly—.01 significance level— with satisfaction, but in the opposite condition. You *still* think it's best to hire the smartest people given the vast body of psychological research.

45. You have as much or more legal liability *after* you hire as you had before.

46. Company Acme Business hires about 30% of their white applicants and 26% of their black applicants. The Human Resources Director maintains her "numbers are good."

47. You have one multiple regression equation with two variables (test measures) that are added to predict driving success. You have another equation that has 13 variables. The multiple R related to the equation with only two variables is more likely to show shrinkage.

48. Your test of musical ability correlates with three other tests of musical ability. You claim this shows some convergent validity.

49. It's a good idea to use selection procedures that look reasonable and appear to have a good logical basis.

50. You have a test that has 12 years of solid information backing it up and a relatively new test. You have supervisors rate the 30 employees they like least and those they like best; the new test does a better job of predicting your rating criterion. You should go with the new test.

Scoring Key Test 1

1.	F	26.	F
2.	F	27.	T
3.	T	28.	T
4.	T	29.	T
5.	F	30.	T
6.	F	31.	F
7.	F	32.	F
8.	F	33.	T
9.	T	34.	F
10.	F	35.	T
11.	T	36.	F
12.	F	37.	F
13.	F	38.	F
14.	T	39.	F
15.	F	40.	F
16.	T	41.	T
17.	T	42.	T
18.	F	43.	T
19.	F	44.	F
20.	F	45.	T
21.	T	46.	T
22.	T	47.	F
23.	T	48.	T
24.	F	49.	T
25.	T	50.	F

Interpretation

50	A+	Great! You have an excellent overview of testing.
45–49	A	Excellent! You have a good grasp of testing. Now pick up the few items you missed and you'll be even better.
40–44	B	You know a lot about testing, but you need to brush up in some areas.
25–39	C	You probably know something about testing, but you have some gaps in your knowledge. Read the pertinent sections, and you can fill in those gaps.

Explanatory Key Test One

1. **FALSE**—EEOC guidelines refers to selection devices as anything that is used to make an employment decision. By EEOC standards, an interview is a test, an application blank is a test, and so forth. Read chapters 1 and 8.

2. **FALSE**—Read chapter 6. The Wechsler Adult Intelligence Scale is a test of general intelligence for adults and yields an IQ score.

3. **TRUE**—Read chapter 4. Empirical means you actually observed real-world data as opposed to basing your decision on abstract logic or some statistical process.

4. **TRUE**—Read chapter 2. This reliability is often determined by having people take the test at one time and later take the test or an equivalent form at another, to see how closely each person scores to his/her prior score.

5. **FALSE**—Read chapter 6. Biodata refers to information about the individual's life such as birth order, previous jobs, and so forth.

6. **FALSE**—Read chapter 2. In the first place it is practically impossible to have a zero false positive rate. Furthermore, if you act to increase the hit rate you will increase false positives!

7. **FALSE**—Read chapter 10. So-called culture fair tests often discriminate as much or more than traditional verbal tests.

8. **FALSE**—Read chapter 2. Statistical significance refers to the likelihood that a difference occurred by chance. For example, a correlation that is significant at the .01 level means that if the measures were not related, a correlation of that size with that sample size would occur about 1 out of a 100 times.

9. **TRUE**—Read chapter 3. Content validity means the validity of the test is based on the fact that the test is representative of critical parts of the actual job.

10. **FALSE**—Read chapter 3. Criterion valid refers to a demonstration that the test predicts some objective criterion or measure of job success. An argument based on theory is a construct validation approach.

11. **TRUE**—Read chapter 5. A multiple cutoff method is best when one measure or ability does not compensate for the other.

12. **FALSE**—Read chapter 2. A correlation is not a percentage of anything. The square of the correlation gives percentage of variance accounted for, but even that is more abstract than it sounds. Don't use correlations as interchangeable with any percentage.

13. **FALSE**—Read chapter 4. The factor analytic approach is a statistical technique to see what items "clump" in a correlational sense. The selection of test items based on expert judgment alone is a rational approach.

14. **TRUE**—Read chapter 8. Negligent hiring is one of the reasons you don't "play it safe" by making lax selection standards.

15. **FALSE**—Read chapter 6. The five factors are: extraversion (which is primarily sociability); neuroticism (nervousness is one of the expressions of neuroticism); openness to new ideas; agreeableness; conscientiousness. Sense of humor may derive from a combination of sociable, open to new ideas and being well adjusted, or it may be a product of many different factors. In any event, it is not a primary personality factor.

16. **TRUE**—Read chapter 2. The square root of the reliability is the highest the validity can be. So if reliability equals .64, the limit of validity is .80 (.80 x .80 = .64).

17. **TRUE**—Read chapter 2. The square root of the reliability is the *limit* for validity, but validity could be lower.

18. **FALSE**—False on every level. Tests are not always required to be validated. In any case, the EEOC gives guidelines for validation and never validates anything. Read chapter 8. *Valid* means nothing unless it is valid relative to some use. Read chapter 3.

19. **FALSE**—Read chapter 8. In general, a test need not be validated if no adverse impact is occurring.

20. **FALSE**—Read chapter 8. An employer may use a test that discriminates against a racial group if the test is valid, that is, if the discrimination is a side effect of business necessity.

21. **TRUE**—See chapter 8. It is generally not necessary to show that every selection component is valid, and it is never sufficient that one component of the selection procedure is valid—the overall procedure is what counts.

22. **TRUE**—See chapter 2. A score is at the xth percentile of a norm group if it is higher than x% of the scores in the norm group.

23. **TRUE**—See chapter 6. A cognitive test is one that measures thinking and problem-solving ability as opposed to interests, personality, or some assessment of emotion.

24. **FALSE**—If John scores 6 out of 20 correct, 6 is his raw score, not the percentile. See chapter 2.

25. **TRUE**—The mode is the most frequently occurring score. See chapter 2.

26. **FALSE**—Read chapter 5. If there are a large number of cases and good data, an actuarial approach is likely to be more accurate than a clinical approach.

27. **TRUE**—Read chapter 10. People usually don't fake tests, and the ability to fake is itself related to positive adjustment.

28. **TRUE**—Read chapters 8 and 9. And hardly surprising, since it's subjectivity and inconsistency make it a ready engine for discrimination. The only surprise is that it hasn't been more frequently challenged.

29. **TRUE**—Read chapter 6. The SCII is a well-known test of vocational interest along with the VPI and SDS.

30. **TRUE**—Read chapter 8. So very true. Anyone can sue you. And measures you take to protect the job applicant may lead to problems in not taking measures to avoid negligent hiring.

31. **FALSE**—Read chapter 10. So obviously false, once you think of it. Yet, how many people act as though the mean old test keeps people from getting jobs?

32. **FALSE**—One of the problems with biodata as a predictor is that life history items (father's occupation, length of time in previous residence) are likely to discriminate against different ethnic and racial groups. Read chapter 6.

33. **TRUE**—Thank goodness, the courts realize that the guidelines are intended to be just that. Employers are not exempted from using common sense. Nevertheless, it is best to TRY HARD to stay within the guidelines. Read chapter 8.

34. **FALSE**—Read chapter 1 and chapter 8. Everything an employer does to select people is a test—there is no way to avoid testing in an EEOC sense. If there were, EEOC would be totally powerless to stop discrimination!

35. **TRUE**—Nonsignificance does not mean equality. With a sample as small as 10 people per group there could be a large difference that the test would fail to detect. If there were no difference with 1,000 people per group, a statistician could make an indirect argument about what that meant, but with small samples in particular, lack of significance may mean nothing. Read chapter 2.

36. **FALSE**—A test can't just be "valid." It has to be valid for a specified population relative to some criterion or measure of success. Read chapter 3.

37. **FALSE**—Supervisory ratings can be flawed, subjective, and discriminatory, more suspect themselves than any test. Read chapter 3 about validity and about supervisory ratings being challenged.

38. **FALSE**—Sales volume may be objective, but it is not always the best measure of sales ability as any VP of Sales can tell you. If Mary is a great salesperson, I may put her in a tough store—so she sells less this quarter than Fred. But Fred is in a plum store where he should be selling even more. Read chapter 3.

39. **FALSE**—Increasing test length has some effect on validity, but the increase is not great even if you triple the test length. In addition, lengthening the test may lead to problems with fatigue. Read chapter 2.

40. **FALSE**—That is a content valid component, but the overall selection procedure is not content valid because the company is not testing the other important components. A person with good typing skills and poor people skills might be hired, and a person with good people skills and poor typing might not—even though greeting people is an important part of the job that actually involves twice as much of the day! See chapter 3.

41. **TRUE**—That is what invasive means. By the same token, if a question does have bearing on the job, asking it is not invasive. Would you consider it invasive to find out if your baby-sitter had a previous record of child molestation? See chapter 10.

42. **TRUE**—Remember, the result could be a fluke 5% of the time. This might be that one-in-twenty roll of the dice. In addition, that's an awfully small sample—perhaps it's not representative. In addition, how can you be sure the ratings were accurate? Don't start hiring police with low stress ratings! Read chapter 3.

43. **TRUE**—It is possible that sports-minded men are more physically active and strong, a skill that transfers to the job of loading and unloading shelves. But that might not be the case at all for strong women. Don't let impressive data push you into doing something that doesn't make sense. Read chapter 3.

44. **FALSE**—It is true that intelligence is a plus in most jobs, including most sales jobs, but that's just not the case here. You have a large sample and good criteria. Gadget may have a product that is simple to understand, and intelligence just isn't much of a factor. In fact, the salesperson satisfaction makes it appear that the very bright people get dissatisfied with the job. Don't let your personal biases get in the way. And as for sharp-looking—that's not the job. Read chapter 3.

45. **TRUE**—You continue to be liable for the basis for promotion and discharge decisions. Read chapter 8.

46. **TRUE**—This hiring rate is consistent with the four-fifths rule of thumb because $.8 \times .3 = .24$ and at .26 Acme is within range. If the difference persists it would still be a good idea to examine why is persists. Read chapter 8.

47. **FALSE**—The more variables, the more likely the equation is to show shrinkage. See chapter 2.

48. **TRUE**—Convergent validity means the measure is related to other similar measures. See chapter 3.

49. **TRUE**—Yes, there are lecturers who will inform you that law is concerned with results and not intentions. In the first place, law is not the only driving factor; you want to appear reasonable in order to avoiding alienating your job candidates. In the second place, judges and juries are human, and they look at intentions whether they should or not. And it's certainly a factor that attorneys look at in deciding to take a case. See chapter 8.

50. **FALSE**—You'll be in trouble if you do! Performance ratings may be valuable or they may be subjective devices that simply put prejudice down in black and white. A bad criterion is not necessarily better than none at all. See chapter 3.

Self-Test 2

1. Culture fair tests give equivalent scores for whites and minorities.

2. It is crucial to remember that an interview is not considered a test by EEOC guidelines.

3. The Rorschach is a self-report personality inventory that can be scored easily by clerical staff.

4. A test item "I like art" is included in a creativity scale. We have no evidence that links liking art to any outside criterion, but it seems logical that it would be—we're using this test item based on a rational approach.

5. Unless you change the test, increasing "hit" rate will probably increase the "false positive" rate as well.

6. Significant at .05 level means that your test result would occur less than 5 out of 100 times simply due to chance.

7. Your studies show that people who say "yes" to the question "do you like green cars" tend to be better computer programmers—you have no idea why. You choose to use this item in a test battery based on a rational approach because of the item's content.

8. Biodata might include things such as birth order and number of previous jobs.

9. You find a test is correlated with a criterion and is significant exactly at the .01 level. You estimate that if 200 researchers did the same study, 2 of them would probably get your results even if there was no real correlation.

10. You have one test that measures speed of learning and another that measures sociability. Regardless of how bright people are, they must be sociable. No matter how sociable they are, they must be able to learn at a certain level. You elect NOT to use a multiple cutoff method of test use, but instead, add the scores.

11. You have a correlation of .50 between measure 1 and measure 2. That means that if you use measure 1 (a test, for example) to predict measure 2 (some measure of success, for example) you may as well flip a coin.

12. In order to avoid legal hassles, your only selection procedure is "high school diploma" required. Since your job obviously requires reading and writing ability, this is a very valid alternative to a test.

13. I am creating a test of anxiety. I created a pool of items that ask about worry, fear, and so forth, and I then used a statistical technique to see which items tend to "go together" whether they refer directly or indirectly to anxiety. Some of the items are obviously related to anxiety, and some are not. I am using a factor-analytic approach to test development.

14. You select Mary Smith for a job that involves handling money for clients. She steals the clients' money and skips out. In court you successfully defend yourself by pointing out that you had no right to invade Mary's privacy— her individual rights certainly come before those of clients.

15. The five factors most commonly identified in the assessment of personality are: sociability; neuroticism; cooperativeness; openness to new ideas; conscientiousness.

16. If the reliability of a test is .64, the validity can be no higher than .70.

17. If the reliability of a test is .66, the validity could be .33.

18. The EEOC does not validate tests.

19. If you use a test in an employment setting, it must be validated for EEOC purposes only if there is adverse impact.

20. An employer may not use a test that discriminates unnecessarily against a racial group.

21. If adverse impact is shown, the employer must show the validity of the portion of his/her selection procedure that involves any standardized testing.

22. I have scores for 10 male managers: 33,34,42,48,50,50,50,51,52,62. The median is 50.

23. A clinical approach involves the judgment of an expert.

24. If a score of 19 is higher than 85% of the scores in that norm group, it is said to be at the 15th percentile.

25. A test that is composed of vocabulary and math items is a cognitive test.

26. John scores 8 out of 24 correct (no correction for guessing), a score that is at the 60th percentile by male college student norms. His raw score is 8.

27. By "playing it safe" your company can be totally assured that it won't be sued for using or not using a selection procedure.

28. To keep your numbers straight, you can simply refuse to hire white males for a while.

29. Unless test items are disguised, people almost always guess their content and fake the test giving a false "healthy" view.

30. The interview is rarely challenged in the courts and is held to a different standard than tests.

31. The Strong Campbell Interest Inventory is a measure of cognitive ability.

32. The Wonderlic Personnel Test is a cognitive test.

33. Courts must follow EEOC Guidelines in ruling on a case.

34. If an expert says a test is "construct valid" all that is required is support for his/her credentials as an expert.

35. Frank does a test to see if blacks score lower than whites. He looks at the scores for 5 black applicants and 5 white applicants and finds a significant difference, with blacks scoring higher. He feels content to use the test. However, as Bill points out, his sample may not be large enough to be representative of the whole population.

36. John, the bank President, is validating his test of Teller ability at several banks using number of customers seen per day as his criterion. He reasons that this is a good measure of how fast people can handle customer needs.

37. The job of secretary at Thatstore, Inc. involves the following important components: 80% typing, 10% filing, 10% miscellaneous. He uses a very realistic typing test and a simulated filing task. He claims his procedure is content valid.

38. The WAIS is a valid test.

39. Supervisory ratings are always accepted by EEOC and the courts as a valid criterion.

40. Even a short test can have good validity.

41. Asking questions about drinking and drug usage are unnecessarily invasive for any job.

42. Experienced professionals such as police investigators invariably learn to detect lies at a very high degree of accuracy.

43. After a year or so of interviewing, practically anyone can learn to effectively learn to read body language and practically read the interviewee's mind.

44. It makes sense that people have to be detail oriented in whatever job they do. I find a test that predicts many criteria related to "detail orientation" one that has items that are obviously related to good attention to details. This is a good test to use even though I don't have a large enough sample of people to validate the test locally.

45. You have just taken over the Human Resources Manager position. You don't want to use testing because of legal liability, so you emphasize the need for managers to rely on experience and education requirements in making all decisions.

46. You are helping Scientific Whiz, Inc. hire engineers. You know, and SW knows, that good engineers are smart. More to the point, your engineers have to design and test products, and all of their work involves mathematics. In your validation study with 200 engineers you use production quality (as assessed by Quality Control) and on-time completion as your criteria. You use three tests, and the math test correlates highest; and it is a significant correlation. The items on the math test are very similar to the types of math that the engineers use on a day-to-day basis. You still feel that a math test is unfair, because women tend to score lower, and women are obviously as good at engineering as men.

47. Company Acme Business hires about 30% of their white applicants and 15% of their black applicants. The Human Resources Director maintains he or she is following the EEOC "one-half rule of thumb."

48. Any criterion validity study is better than none at all.

49. You have a test battery with 35 different scores. The Multiple R is .50. Since you have a large sample of people, you can be sure your result won't "shrink" in future applications.

50. Your test of math ability correlates with math measures but not as strongly with other measures of verbal and clerical ability measures. You claim this shows discriminant validity.

Scoring Key Test 2

1.	F	26.	T
2.	F	27.	F
3.	F	28.	F
4.	T	29.	F
5.	T	30.	F
6.	T	31.	F
7.	F	32.	T
8.	T	33.	F
9.	T	34.	F
10.	F	35.	T
11.	F	36.	F
12.	F	37.	T
13.	T	38.	F
14.	F	39.	F
15.	T	40.	T
16.	F	41.	F
17.	T	42.	F
18.	T	43.	F
19.	T	44.	F
20.	T	45.	F
21.	F	46.	F
22.	T	47.	F
23.	T	48.	F
24.	F	49.	F
25.	T	50.	T

Interpretation

50	A+	Great! You have an excellent overview of testing.
45–49	A	Excellent! You have a good grasp of testing. Now pick up the few items you missed and you'll be even better.
40–44	B	You know a lot about testing, but you need to brush up in some areas.
25–39	C	You probably know something about testing, but you have some gaps in your knowledge. Read the pertinent sections and you can fill in those gaps.

Explanatory Key Test 2

1. **FALSE**—On so-called culture fair tests African–Americans usually score lower than whites. See chapter 10.

2. **FALSE**—An interview (or any other selection device) is legally a test. See chapters 1, 8, and 9.

3. **FALSE**—The Rorschach is a projective personality test whose scoring is very complex and usually requires professional interpretation. See chapter 6.

4. **TRUE**—Inclusion of test items based on judgment is a rational approach as opposed to factor-analytic or empirical. See chapter 4.

5. **TRUE**—For example, if you lower a cut score to be sure of not missing good students who happen to score low, you will also select more bad students. See chapter 1.

6. **TRUE**—Significant at .05 level means that your test result would occur less than 5 out of 100 times simply due to chance. See chapter 2.

7. **FALSE**—The content has nothing to do with computer programming. You are using an empirical approach. See chapter 4.

8. **TRUE**—Biodata might include such things as birth order and number of previous jobs. See chapter 6.

9. **TRUE**—Significant at the .01 level means the result would occur only 1 out of 100 times if there were no real relationship. For example, you would estimate that if 200 researchers did the same study, 2 of them would probably get your results even if there was no real correlation. See chapter 2.

10. **FALSE**—You should use multiple cutoff, because neither score in any way compensates for the other. See chapter 5.

11. **FALSE**—A correlation of .50 is not the same as a probability. And remember, fifty-fifty is chance level only for two-outcome events, like a coin. Fifty percent is well above chance for rolling seven two times in a row. See chapter 2.

12. **FALSE**—In the first place, education requirements are tests. See chapter 1, and also see chapter 8. In the second place there may be far better ways to assess reading and writing.

13. **TRUE**—You are using a factor-analytic approach. See chapter 4.

14. **FALSE**—You indeed have a responsibility to be fair in hiring Mary Smith, but you cannot respect her rights at the expense of the public you serve. See chapter 8.

15. **TRUE**—The five factors most commonly identified in the assessment of personality are: sociability, neuroticism, cooperativeness, openness to new ideas, and conscientiousness. See chapter 6.

16. **FALSE**—If the reliability of a test is .64, the validity can be no higher than .80. See chapter 2.

17. **TRUE**—If the reliability of a test is .66, the validity could be .33. See chapter 2.

18. **TRUE**—EEOC does provide guidelines for validation. See chapter 8.

19. **TRUE**—In general, EEOC action is triggered only by adverse impact. See chapter 8.

20. **TRUE**—The key is "unnecessary discrimination." If most white males are excluded by a selection procedure that is job related and no better alternative is available, that discrimination is unfortunate but necessary. If discrimination were never allowed, there would be no need for validation guidelines. See chapter 8.

21. **FALSE**—The employer must show the validity of the overall process; it is generally not necessary and never sufficient to examine only one part, testing or otherwise. See chapter 8.

22. **TRUE**—The median score is higher than 50% and lower than 50% of the scores—right in the middle. See chapter 2.

23. **TRUE**—A clinical approach involves the judgment of an expert. See chapter 5.

24. **FALSE**—If a score of 19 is higher than 85% of the scores in that norm group, it is said to be at the 85th percentile, not the 15th. See chapter 2.

25. **TRUE**—Tests of reasoning, learning, and thinking are cognitive tests. See chapter 6.

26. **TRUE**—The raw score is the actual score before it is "normed." See chapter 2.

27. **FALSE**—There is no sure way to "play it safe." See chapter 8.

28. **FALSE**—In some situations you may use race or gender as one factor to remedy past wrongs, but you cannot violate the rights of any group, minority, or majority. See chapter 8.

29. **FALSE**—Some people can fake tests with obvious items, in practice most people don't. See chapter 10.

30. **FALSE**—The interview is a test by EEOC standards (see chapter 1) and has been challenged in court and has been found wanting in many cases (see chapters 8 and 9).

31. **FALSE**—The Strong Campbell Interest Inventory is a measure of vocational interests. See chapter 6.

32. **TRUE**—Read about the Wonderlic Personnel Test in chapter 6.

33. **FALSE**—See chapter 8.

34. **FALSE**—It is NOT enough to say someone is an expert to support "construct validity." See chapter 3.

35. **TRUE**—In theory, a significant result with a small sample is very meaningful. But such a small sample might not be representative of the populations of black and white workers. See chapter 2 and also see chapter 3.

36. **FALSE**—The criterion could be affected by many variables besides ability as a Teller. If challenged due to adverse impact, the plaintiff could validly point out that the criterion could have been affected by bank location, that "seeing a lot of people" might not be a good standard. Perhaps the bad Tellers were abrupt and see a lot of people at the expense of long-term relationships. Even if not challenged, why base your hiring on something that doesn't really gauge success? See chapter 3.

37. **TRUE**—His test samples the major content of the job. See chapter 3.

38. **FALSE**—It can't just be "valid." It is not valid as a measure of musical ability; it is not valid as a test of truck driving knowledge; and so forth. See chapter 3.

39. **FALSE**—Supervisory ratings are NOT always accepted by EEOC as a valid criterion—they may be more discriminatory than any test. See chapter 3.

40. **TRUE**—Length is a factor in validity, but not a major one. See chapter 2.

41. **FALSE**—If you're going to hire someone to fly a commercial plane or be in charge of children, NOT asking questions about drinking and drug usage may violate the rights of the public those people are to serve. Read about negligent hiring in chapter 8 and also see chapter 10.

42. **FALSE**—Even experts do not have people reading skills in areas such as integrity to the degree some people think—they often act at chance level. See chapter 9.

43. **FALSE**—See the explanation above for item 42 and read chapter 9.

44. **FALSE**—Look at your assumption that "it makes sense that people have to be detail oriented in whatever job they do." Why does that make sense? Don't assume it's required. See chapter 3.

45. **FALSE**—Education and experience requirements are tests in a legal sense. See chapters 1 and 8.

46. **FALSE**—You have good reasons to assume the content and construct is correct. You have a good sample size. If women score lower than men (or vice versa) it may be unfortunate but it's not unfair. See chapters 3 and 8.

47. **FALSE**—There is a "four-fifths" rule of thumb, but there is no "one-half rule of thumb." See chapter 8.

48. **FALSE**—A poor criterion validity study is far worse than simply relying on common sense. See chapters 3 and 8.

49. **FALSE**—Shrinkage is a function of sample size *and* number of predictors. See chapter 2.

50. **TRUE**—Discriminant validity means the test does not correlate as highly with measures that should have less relationship. See chapter 3.

CHAPTER NOTES

Chapter 1

Certainly standardized tests are legally liable. Critics of testing will cite cases such as *Griggs v. Duke Power Company* (1971), *United States v. Georgia Power Company* (1973), and *Connecticut v. Teal* (1982), showing that testing has been determined invalid in some situations. In those cases the concern was not with the tests, but rather the way in which they were used and/or supporting evidence for the way they were used. In *Soroka v. Dayton Hudson* (1991), the test itself was condemned as unnecessarily invasive for the specific situation.

But, having reviewed such cases and pertinent law, it is vital to remember that *all other selection devices are tests*. The interview in particular, is a test and has been found often wanting in the courts as unsupported and inherently flawed. Read chapter 9 and the accompanying chapter notes carefully to see the many examples. Read *all* of the Uniform Guidelines of 1978, especially the definition of "selection procedure." In addition, call your local EEOC office for additional information on hiring, including information about Americans With Disabilities Act.

Chapter 2

Increasing Test Length

The relative unimportance of test length in a test that is valid has long been known. Cronbach (1960, p.367) points out that the only importance of reliability is its effect on validity: "In a test intended for predicting a definite criterion, reliability is less important than predictive validity. If predictive validity is satisfactory, low reliability does not discourage us from using the test." The importance of reliability is its limiting effect on validity—and that effect isn't much. Ruch and Ruch (1963, p.3) use the Spearman-Brown formula to illustrate changes in test validity and reliability as a function of increasing length. A test with validity of .40 with 10 items would have .43 with 20 items, and .48 with 20 billion items! They point out that "...unique tests combined in a battery may be considerably reduced in length and their reliabilities consequently lowered without appreciable decrease in composite validity." Guilford (1950) also agrees that given a choice between lengthening a test to increase reliability or adding more tests to broaden validity the latter is the better alternative.

The Correlation

Elsewhere I have argued (Rose, 1984) that we should use probabilities instead of correlations where possible. I doubt we will see any less use of the correlation in the near future.

Misunderstanding of Variance Accounted For

People will frequently mistake the correlation for a probabililty and will think that a correlation of .40 means something about 40%. The squared correlation does refer to "variance accounted for" and, unfortunately, that is often misinterpreted. Seymour (1988, p. 358) is quoted frequently in this book because he is so outspoken with such incorrect arguments, variance accounted for being yet another example. He says at one point: "...surely, none of us would invest his or her $10,000 based on a program which predicted only 4% or 9% or 16% of the variability in stock prices." Seymour does not point out what stock prediction is equal to a .40 correlation, much less better, but apparently he feels that most stock investors do. Obviously, he feels that "only 16%" has some meaning. Researchers working with data rather than hypothetical stock market predictors (see Campbell, 1991) point out that even small correlations can have a significant and positive effect on practical prediction. Gordon, Lewis, and Quigley (1988, p. 430) provide a realistic perspective on supposedly small correlations.

In some cases you can overcome the difficulties of explaining correlations by recasting the data (when available) into an expectancy table. The GRE Advanced Chemistry Test correlates .39 with completion of the Ph.D. (see Willingham, 1974 as discussed in Anastasi, 1976, pp. 322–323). That's a large correlation considering that graduate students present a very restricted range! Nevertheless, the GRE accounts for only about 15% of the variance. Does that mean it doesn't do much, I mean 15%...?

Let's look at the relevant data in an expectancy table.

GRE Stanine	Percentage completing Ph.D. (%)
8–9	75–80%
4–5	50–55%
1–2	25–30%

The table tells us that 75% of the students scoring above the eighth stanine on the GRE completed the Ph.D.; less than 30% of the students scoring 2 or lower did so. If you were predicting graduate success wouldn't you consider those numbers meaningful?

And by the way, let me say in all seriousness, if any reader finds a stock market predictor that correlates .40—or even predicts as well as the .39 correlation in the example above—call me. But hurry! A lot of people will want to know about a stock market predictor which can change the odds from 25/75 to 75/25!

Chapter 3

What's the Best Form of Validity?

The problems with criterion-related validity

The Uniform Guidelines §14D indicates: "Construct validity is a more complex strategy than either criterion-related or content validity..." Miner and Miner (1978, p. 85) argued that the standards for construct validity were such as to make its use meaningless. But even in 1978 the problems with this "less complex" strategy of criterion validity, (e.g., sample size, criteria) were pointed out in the Uniform Guidelines.

Time and experience have shown that the problems associated with criterion-related validity are many. As Campbell (1990, p. 721) points out: "In the work force as a whole, most forecasts of future performance must be made in the absence of criterion-based empirical prediction rules. Relatively speaking, we simply don't have very many criterion-related validation studies. Further, a poor study (e.g., in terms of criterion measurement) may be worse than no study at all for parameter estimation, and even a good study may be misleading if it has low statistical power." The American Psychological Association concurs. The *American Psychological Association Standards* point out that "...it may be better to try and investigate criterion-related validity, even if imperfectly, than to accept totally untested hypotheses. However, 'doing something' is not necessarily better than doing nothing; the results of an inadequate study may be quite misleading. Results of validation studies with severely restricted ranges or small Ns are especially open to question."

Sample size. Concerns about sample size are simply a matter of straightforward statistics. Schmidt, Hunter, Croll, and McKenzie (1983) went a step further and looked at sample size relative to expert opinion. They found that it would take a sample of 90 cases to equal 1 judge and continued: "The sample size required to match 4 judges is 324. The sample size required to equal the accuracy of 10 judges is 673. These sample sizes are far larger than the typical validation study size of 68 (Lent, Aurbach, & Levin, 1971, p. 596). "Thus, we conclude that judgments of validity by experts can contain substantially more information than is contained in and yielded by many local criterion-related validity studies." Hollenbeck and Whitener (1988) also point out the difficulty of getting a large enough sample size for criterion validity studies. When you stop to consider that more than 90% of all businesses (Kunde, 1992) employ less than 20 people, the sample size problem becomes quite real.

One comment: In theory, the problem with small samples is their inability to detect real difference; if, on the other hand, a significant result is found with a small sample, it is quite meaningful. In *theory* if I find a difference between 2 groups of 10 people each, it must be a very powerful difference. In practice, you need to be concerned with how *representative* such a small sample is.

Criterion problems. With regard to the criterion problem, Borman (1991) discusses the difficulty of performance rating as a criterion because raters are limited in their ability to give accurate ratings. And finding "objective" measures is at the very least difficult, or, as Hogan says "...there is probably no such thing as an objective performance measure" (1991, p. 713). This is not merely academic musing—it is a legal issue! In *Rowe v. General Motors* (1972), *Brito v. Zia Company* (1973), *Wade v. Mississippi Cooperative Extension Service* (1974), *Albemarle v. Moody* (1975), and *Watkins v. Scott Paper Co.* (1976), to name a few, the courts found performance ratings—often used as the criterion against which tests are to be validated—to be "tests" which were severely wanting.

This is not to say that criteria—even the subjective measures of performance ratings—should be scrapped. Campbell (1991) and Hogan (1991) point out that performance ratings can have a legitimate place in the workplace. The main point is that merely labeling some measure as a criterion does not automatically give it special status, either theoretically, practically, or legally.

Content validity

In their review of legal cases, Arvey and Faley (1988, p. 172) point out: "The courts have increasingly acknowledged that content validity is an equally acceptable strategy in and of itself, and not just a poor second choice to criterion-related validity." They go on to point out some of the advantages of content validity: "Content validity does not appear to be associated with the thorny psychometric problems of unfair test discrimination or bias that are so much a part of criterion-related studies. Since there is no criterion per se in content validity, underprediction and overprediction, differential validity, and other complexities need not be examined."

One important point: If you're going to defend content validity, remember the word *content*. You must show that the relevant portions of the job were adequately covered. In *Nash v. Jacksonville*, 1990, adverse impact was shown to be related to a promotion exam, and the test was not found to be valid, despite the defendant's claim that the test was job related. Don't allow anyone to cite this case as case history against tests, however; the defendant did not produce the test itself as evidence! The court had little choice.

Also, remember that the content of a seemingly simple behavior may be quite complex. Barrett and Depinet (1991) give the example of driving behavior. McClelland (1973) had said: "if you want to know how well a person can drive a car (the criterion), sample his ability to do so by giving him a driver's test." Sounds good; but Barrett and Depinet reviewed studies (e.g., Edwards, Hahn, & Fleishman, 1977, and several others), which showed that drivers tests did not predict accident involvement or citations received. Why? Perhaps because there are many factors besides driving skill that could be involved in these criteria.

Current psychological thinking—it's all Construct

Despite the early negative views of those who, viewing the Uniform Guidelines, found construct validity virtually impossible to demonstrate (Miner & Miner, 1978) we have come full circle. The current state of affairs is expressed clearly by Campbell (1990, p. 724) who says that many management specialists view construct validity as the overarching strategy in the sense that all inferences made from tests must be supported by evidence bearing on what the scores mean. (See also Dunnette & Borman, 1979; Jones & Appelbaum, 1989; Guion, 1991).

The *Standards for Educational and Psychological Testing* (p. 9) certainly emphasize the current view that validation is a process that involves a mixture of approaches. "Although evidence may be accumulated in many ways, validity always refers to the degree to which that evidence supports the inferences that are made from test scores." As Arvey and Faley (1988) point out "...it should be remembered that the information in the Uniform Guidelines (like that in other EEOC as well as professional guidelines) was not expected to be used as a checklist. For example, as noted in the 1985 APA Standards, assessment of a test's validity 'does not rest in the literal satisfaction of every primary standard in this document p. 8; such assessments are ultimately based on professional judgment *guided* by the material in such documents.'"

Ultimately all validity is construct validity. But, we mustn't imagine that this means that armchair intellectualizing by self-proclaimed experts will replace sound research. Jones and Appelbaum (1989) caution the need to show prediction and/or content sampling if a test is to be well supported in court. Be sure to use good items—for some tests it may be that a purely empirical approach is reasonable, but generally speaking, good tests have good item content. Gormly (1985) discusses the value of good item content, and the *Soroka* case (discussed in chapter 10) may serve as a precedent to demand noninvasive item content.

Be sure to find relevant criteria where at all possible. Goldstein (1991) points out that training success can serve as a criterion if there is solid job-related content in the training.

Also, remember that as McKenna and Wright (1992) remind us, an organization is a growing organism versus a machine! Thus, the criteria for successful performance may change according to the state of the organization and its changing management practices. They cite the work of such people as Bentz (1968) who, in designing *Sears Executive Battery,* considered not only the job but the manner in which the company was growing.

Of greatest importance: Be sure to think about the underlying logic of your test in putting all of these components together. You must be able to *explain* your reasoning.

Not surprisingly, psychology is just catching up with a realization that the physical sciences have had for many years—namely, that there is no "empirical evidence" apart from theory and presupposition.

Judson (1980) in his chapter on "Evidence" quotes Sir Arthur Eddington, who wrote in 1934 "It is also a good rule not to put too much confidence in the observational results that are put forward until they are *confirmed by theory.*" [italics mine] Judson interviewed Paul Dirac, nobel prize winning physicist, about theory and observation, and Dirac stated: "...it's most important to have a beautiful theory. And if the observations don't support it, don't be too distressed, but wait a bit and see if some error in the observations doesn't show up." Hungarian logician and philosopher of science says: "...there is no natural (i.e., psychological) demarcation between observational and theoretical propositions" (Judson, p. 205).

As Judson explains, none of these imminent thinkers have taken leave of their senses but, rather, they realize that observations are made by humans and are hence imperfect. So-called objective observations are always related to some underlying theory or assumptions. To accept a radar reading as objective data is to assume the theory underlying radar is correct. To use body temperature as evidence of health is to assume many physiological theories are correct. To accept sales per month as a criterion is to assume that this is a valid measure of job success. In the field of psychology we are re-creating the wheel to recognize that there is no perfect criterion validity.

Guion (1991, p. 388) sums up the validity question well. He speaks of: "...a paradigmatic shift from reliance on numbers narrowly evaluated to broad-based professional judgment as the essential method of evaluating predictor use." But he makes an important qualification. "Professional judgment, unlike hunch or 'play-it by ear' decision-making, is systematic, informed, and based on understanding and research."

Differential validity

Schmidt (1988) argues that there is no racial differential validity for cognitive tests and that differences that were found were due to chance errors due to small samples. In addition, Arvey and Faley (1988) do an interesting review in which they demonstrate that differential treatment would actually lead to penalizing rather than helping minority candidates.

Validity generalization

Be aware that this is a hot topic, particularly in the area of cognitive tests. Read chapter 3 and especially chapter 10.

Synthetic validity

See Arvey and Faley (1988) for a general discussion and Mossholder and Arvey (1984) for a more detailed discussion.

Chapter 4

Political

Drasgow (1987) discusses two court cases concerning standardized licensing exams. *Golden Rule Insurance Company et al. v. Washburn et al.* (1984) and *Allen v. Alabama State Board of Education* (1985). In both cases, litigation led test developers to agree to try and select only those items which had an equal pass rate for black and white. In what may be a classic understatement, Drasgow notes: "It is important to note that there is no scientific justification for the test construction procedures described; they can only be justified on political grounds." *Soroka v. Dayton Hudson* (1991) is also a case in which individual test items were rejected for being invasive. While focusing on individual test items may not be psychometrically valid, we can have some sympathy with *Soroka*—people should not be made to feel unnecessarily uneasy.

Chapter 5

Actuarial Versus Clinical

To some extent, any debates about these two methods are likely to be sound and fury with very little light. Is clinical always best? Anyone who stops to consider the situation, realizes that a formula will be more consistent than any human judge could ever be. Inwald (1988) gives an example of a situation in which a statistical model of test scores yielded better predictions than the psychologists' interpretations of the score. An actuarial model of a *clinician's own judgment* will be more accurate than the clinician herself—simply because it is more consistent.

Is actuarial always best? No, because we don't have a formula for every occasion. One of the most ardent actuarial supporters, Meehl (1957) stated the case quite clearly: "Mostly we will use our heads, because there just aren't any formulas..."

The actuarial versus clinical discussion is closely related to the discussion of construct versus criterion validity (see chapter 3 and its chapter notes). In both cases we are talking about judgment. That may be the judgment involved in using theory to build a test or the judgment involved in making a clinical decision. In all cases, let's share Guion's (1991) emphasis on the need for professional judgment, with all of the rigor or thinking implied by the word "professional."

Configural Versus Linear

If you don't understand the "all average" profile, work through the illustration below, in which there are two test scales with 1 for the lowest score range (bottom 25%), 2 and 3 the midrange "average" (middle 50%), and 4 the high (top 25%). Total scores of 4 to 6 would represent a sum of average scores.

	Test	
<u>A</u>	<u>B</u>	<u>Total</u>
1	1	2
1	2	3*
1	3	4*
1	4	5*
2	1	3*
2	2	4* x
2	3	5* x
2	4	6*
3	1	4*
3	2	5* x
3	3	6* x
3	4	7
4	1	5*
4	2	6*
4	3	7
4	4	8

As you can see, most of the total scores (12/16 = 75%) are average—those with an asterisk. But the probability of two scores that are both average is only 4/16 or 25%. With three scales only 13% of the population have all three average. Dunnette (1966) discusses some studies (e.g., Lykken & Rose, 1963; Sorenson, 1964) that show configural analyses may be superior in some cases. Yukl and Van Fleet (1992) discuss the trend of viewing leadership traits as a balance, a combination, of traits citing such studies as Zaccarro, Foti, and Kenny (1991), which show the importance of the *combination* of traits in effective managers.

Multiple Cutoff Versus Additive

The term *additive* is sometimes replaced with *linear* or *compensatory*. Remember, the key concept is that in a multiple cutoff situation, you must separately pass each hurdle and in an additive model, one score can add to another and thus compensate.

There is no right answer. Guion (1991) points out that linear, additive models simply work in most cases. He also cites Lord's argument (1962, 1963) that multiple cutoff models assume perfectly reliable tests. On the other hand, Cronbach (1960) points out that while one ability usually compensates for another, that assumption is not always justified. He points out a situation in which men were chosen for Sonar school because their high mechanical comprehension "compensated" for low tonal judgment in their overall score—but it did not compensate for it in actual practice. Thus, in this case, even a test of tonal judgment that was not perfectly reliable should be used in multiple cutoff fashion (as indeed it was used eventually in the Sonar school).

Simple and Mechanical Versus Complex and Clinical

There is one approach that emphasizes adding up the scores and making predictions in a straight line, for example, if 5 is better than 3, 8 will be better than 5. Another camp assumes that some traits don't always add, but must be combined in a more complex way and interpreted in a situational manner. Which way is right? In general, the consistent and mathematical approach will work best—but be aware of the exceptions.

Raw Scores Versus Normed Scores

Since most people consider normed scores automatically the best, the discussion may not come up very often. Some of Holland's materials (e.g., VPI Computer Version, Rose, & Holland, 1985; SDS, Holland, 1979) make use of raw scores. Holland gives a very insightful discussion of this issue in discussing his use of raw scores in the SDS. "I prefer the raw score principle because of its simplicity and low cost. After all, norms are never quite right for a particular client, and they are expensive to develop. I saw later that raw scores have another virtue that traditional normed scores do not: a clear and striking relationship between the score and reality. For example, a Realistic raw score of 24 means that a person has said yes to half of the R items. In contrast, a percentile rank of 50 indicates different raw scores (realities) depending on the norm group used."

Where to Put the Cut Score

Arvey and Faley (1988) discuss several ways to use "cut scores" including racially adjusted quota models (which are no longer legal). Their review makes it clear that cognitive tests are likely to discriminate, fairly or otherwise if a single cut score is used. The Uniform Guidelines have this to say: "The evidence of both the validity and utility of a selection procedure should support the method the user chooses for operational use of the procedure."(§5G) "Where cutoff scores are used, they should normally be set so as to be reasonable and consistent with normal expectations of acceptable proficiency within the work force."(§5H) Be reasonable!

Don't Be Overprecise or Impractical!

As Fearnside and Holther point out (1959, p. 55, p.64) "logic chopping" can be nonsense. To define "bald" as "fewer than 5,000 hairs" makes the definition more precise—but to what end? Using the example of law, the authors discuss the need to avoid curing *unnecessary* vagueness with arbitrary terms. "For example, 'negligence' or the establishment of guilt 'beyond a reasonable doubt' cannot profitably be defined in an arbitrary way. In law as in less rigorous fields there are categories that resist either reduction to particular cases (precedents) or precise definition."

Test Distortions

A good place to get a handle on the perceived importance of these factors comes from the survey reported in *Human Resource Executive* (1992).

Based on a survey of 497 human resources executives the biggest concerns were with test results that were slow in turnaround, inaccurate, contradictory, or filled with jargon. The majority were still positive about testing, nonetheless.

Chapter 6

If you are not a psychologist you may be hampered in your investigation of specific tests because some of the materials will not be sold to nonpsychologists. The research guide (Appendix 1) will point you to sources of information such as *Buros Mental Measurements Yearbook,* which can be found in any good academic library.

Cognitive Tests in General

The WAIS. You can read about the WAIS in many books, including Anastasi (1976) and, of course, the manual (Wechsler, 1981). Incidentally, don't be misled by the date of the manual, that's just the updated version. The test has been around a long time. Wechsler points out that in Buros 8th Mental Measurement Yearbook (1978) there were 1,300 publications concerning the WAIS.

The Wonderlic. *The Wonderlic Personnel Test Manual* (1992) is a good place to start if you want to research this test. The author cites studies showing correlations of .92 between the Wonderlic and the WAIS, along with other supporting research.

Clinical Personality Tests

The MMPI. See Graham (1990) for a discussion of the MMPI-2. As with other manuals, the MMPI has been around for a long time, 1990 is just the latest update of information.

Normal Personality Tests

The NEO Manual (Costa & McCrae, 1985) will give you a good description of this exemplary test. The authors give normative information, describe the development of the test, and show its relationship to established tests such as the Guilford Zimmerman Temperament Survey (1976, see discussion of the power of this test in chapter notes for chapter 10) and the Vocational Preference Inventory (1985). If you cannot obtain the manual, get the journal citation for the following articles, which you can find in the library: Costa and McCrae (1984), Costa, McCrae, and Holland (1984), and Schroeder and Costa (1984). The 16 PF manual (Caltell, Eber, & Tetsuoka, 1970) contains some interesting data.

Projective Techniques

Hogan (1991) has some interesting information about the use of projectives in industry.

Interest Inventories

Holland's book *Making Vocational Choices* (1985), will give you a good understanding of modern vocational theory. In addition, you can write to test publishers (see chapter 14) for a list of tests and their manuals. The manuals for the VPI (Holland, 1985) and the SCII (Hansen & Campbell, 1985) contain solid supporting data.

Biodata

See Mumford and Owens (1987) for a review of research on biodata. Some researchers are very enthusiastic about biodata (e.g., Drakeley, Herriot & Jones, 1988; Guion, 1991) but others have serious concerns. Some researchers (e.g., McCormick & Ilgen, 1980; Thayer, 1977) point out that societal changes may lead to changes in relevancy of biodata items. Bass and Barrett (1981) voice the most serious concern: that very effective biodata items such as age, marital status, and occupation of father, will be discriminatory and should be avoided. I agree with Bass and Barrett. In theory, you might be able to demonstrate empirically that "occupation of father" predicted a job criteria; in practice, you would have an uphill battle proving that this was less discriminatory than other alternatives; I doubt that the hassle would be worth the gain.

Chapter 7

Don't disparage Mom and Pop businesses! Remember that 91% of all businesses employ less than 20 employees (Kunde, 1992).

Chapter 8

Your best bet for more in-depth discussion of all issues covered in this chapter will be Arvey and Faley (1988). This book contains discussions of EEOC, Affirmative Action, and case law.

The Spirit of EEOC

In a recent lawsuit (see Pulley, 1992) a company was alleged to have covertly used a darkened letter on the application blank to indicate African–American applicants. That information was then used allegedly to discriminate based on race. This is an example of the practices the EEOC is designed to guard against.

Affirmative Action

It's a great idea, but handle with care. One negative view was expressed by Thernstrom in a recent *Wall Street Journal* article: "In an affirmative action setting, white signifies 'competent' while black denotes 'needs help.' No facts uncovered in the course of an inquiry can possibly calm the anguish and anger among both blacks and whites that the message brings."

Americans with Disabilities Act

Information cited is from materials from ADA Texas, Texas Rehabilitation Commission, Austin, Texas. Get a copy of PL 101-336 Americans with Disabilities Act of 1990 if you wish to read more about all aspects of ADA.

The Guidelines are guidelines

As mentioned in the section "Experts don't agree," the court does not always follow guidelines. In 1988, p. 312, Arvey and Faley predicted: "The existing case law indicates that the various sets of EEOC-issued guidelines will not be automatically accorded 'great deference.' "

It's best to read the guidelines, read other sources of pertinent information, and contract a psychologist with strong credentials.

Unions

There are certainly cases in which tests can be used. In *Great Lakes Chemical Corp.* (1990) the plaintiff argued that tests were used to detect union attitudes. The court said that the tests were: (1) widely used in business, (2) were not the sole basis for decision-making, and, (3) not necessary to determine union feelings and were therefore lawfully used.

You Can't Play it Safe

You can't protect yourself with empty files!

In the Uniform Guidelines, §15 tells you about record keeping. In addition, you might be challenged in other ways (e.g., negligent hiring), and you'll want records that indicate what you did was right.

Anyone can sue you

One organization sued a company that had developed a selection device, saying that the selection device had caused discrimination. The company that produced the selection device succeeded in having the case dismissed by showing that the discrimination was caused by factors other than the test. (BNA's *Employee Relations Weekly*, May 18, 1992) It's good to be able to defend yourself, but potentially quite costly even if you win. It's simply a risk you have to face.

Negligent hiring and respondeat superior

Respondeat superior refers to an employer's responsibility in cases where employees cause harm because of their inability to perform the job they were hired for. Negligent hiring is even broader in definition. A cogent, and frightening, review by Ryan and Lasek (1991) will give you a great deal of information about just how vulnerable an employer can be by not gathering enough information. Attorney Edward Mitchell of the Labor and Employment Law Department of Thompson, Hine, and Flory makes the following point about testing: "The theory behind this expanding area of litigation is that if the employer had been more careful in the hiring process, the employee who causes the injury would not have been hired and, therefore, would not have been in a position to commit the wrong. Unlike other potential areas for litigation involving testing, testing in this area may provide a *defense* and failure to test may arguably expose an employer to liability."

Hiring is not your only area of liability

In recruiting, you can have problems. In *EEOC v. Detroit Edison* (1975) the practice of relying on referrals by a predominantly white workforce was ruled discriminatory. Once you have hired, promotion and discharge decisions can lead to even more liability. Lublin (1991) writing for the *Wall Street Journal* points out: "But comparatively few people complain about allegedly unfair hiring these days. Nearly 61% of the bias charges filed with the Equal Employment Opportunity Commission in fiscal 1990 targeted advancement and discharge decisions. Only 8.6% aimed at hiring." Also, see the sections on negligent hiring.

The experts don't agree

Tenopyor and Oeltjen (1982) examined the Uniform Guidelines and the *Principles for the Validation and Use of Personnel Selection Procedures* (American Psychological Association Division of Industrial and Organizational Psychology, 1980) and found that, far from being in perfect agreement, there were seven areas of sharp variance. For example: the *Principles* express no preference for validation strategy while the Uniform Guidelines express a preference for criterion-related validity; the *Principles* emphasize validation *strategies* rather than the rigid division implied in the Uniform Guidelines. The authors state: "Thus, it appears that serious controversy between professional standards and guidelines and misunderstandings about what is required in a validation effort will be possible in legal proceedings."

Attorneys can take advantage of this confusion. Gordon, Lewis, and Quiqley (1988) review an article by Attorney Seymour (1988) in which he lists ways in which plaintiffs can successfully challenge validity generalization. The authors find Seymour's challenges flawed but concede that they can "pay off"—"That such scientifically flawed efforts may proceed from good intentions, and sometimes pay off in court (e.g., Larry P.) does not lessen their corrosiveness to public morale or the long-range risks to race relations and major institutions when they succeed in misdirecting public policy."

Sharf (1988, p. 265) complains that the EEOC is sometimes guilty of "...construing the law to its own self-appointed agenda." Whether this is true or not, one thing is very clear: the courts are not bound by guidelines. As Kleiman and Faley (1985) point out in their review of court cases, judges tend to sidestep technical issues and rely on common sense. Their observations are certainly borne out by some court decisions. In *Spurlock v. United Airlines* (1972) a black male was denied employment because he did not have a college degree. Keep in mind that an educational requirement is legally a test, a test that historically discriminates against minorities. And, Arvey (1979) and Arvey and Faley (1988) point out the validation of an educational requirement is quite difficult. The court nevertheless upheld the requirement as did a subsequent court of appeals.

In *Blake v. the City of Los Angeles* (1977) it was argued that the city had not validated its employment practices in the manner recommended by the EEOC regulations. The court disregarded the guidelines and stated: "There is no magic in any validating procedure, and the defendants need only supply competent and relevant evidence in this issue." (See Arvey and Faley, 1988, for discussion of these and other cases).

In *Watson v. Fort Worth Bank and Trust* (1988), also discussed in Sharf (1988), Justice O'Connor wrote: "...our cases make it clear that employers are not required, even when defending standardized or objective tests, to introduce formal validation studies showing that particular criteria predict actual on-the-job performance." In reviewing *Watson*, Bolick (1988) says: "The plurality rejected mechanical reliance upon the EEOC guidelines or any other rigid formula." (*Watson* led to some other changes, which have since been reinstated by the Civil Rights Act of 1991).

In short, the Uniform Guidelines and the standards of the psychological community are not in agreement. In addition, the courts are not bound to follow any set of rigid guidelines but may—indeed do—use common sense.

While the confusion of different sources of guidance is frustrating, the ability of courts to use sound judgment is often encouraging. For example, the courts often take into account the seriousness of making a bad hire. In their review of court cases, Arvey and McGowan (1983) found that experience requirements were more likely to be upheld for jobs that were complex and where mis-hires could lead to economic risks or other risks. This principle can be generalized in other areas. In *Chrisner v. Compete Auto Transit, Inc.* (1981) the court affirmed: "...when the job clearly requires a high degree of skill and the economic and human risks involved in hiring an unqualified applicant are great, the employer bears a correspondingly lighter burden to show that his employment criteria are job related."

The courts often take reality into account in evaluating hiring criteria, as in the case of *Rogers v. International Paper Company* (1975), in which the court said: "Subjective criteria are not to be condemned as unlawful per se, for in all fairness to applicants and employers alike, decisions about hiring and promotion in supervisory and managerial jobs cannot realistically be made using objective standards alone."

Bottom line: Courts can follow guidelines or not, make decisions, which could be overthrown by a series of higher courts, and Congress can always enact new legislation.

You cannot discriminate against one group to be fair to another

You can't negatively impact the majority to help the minority (see the discussion of Affirmative Action). In *McDonald v. Santa Fe Trail Transportation Company* (1976), the Supreme Court stated: "It's [Title VII] terms are not limited to the discrimination against members of any particular race." The court said law prohibits "...discriminatory preference for any (racial) group, minority or majority." *Regents of the University of California v. Bakke* (1978) affirmed the unlawfulness of reverse discrimination. In *Watson v. Fort Worth Bank and Trust* (1988), the plurality emphasizes that Title VII was not designed to encourage the use of quotas. Greve (1992) discusses the fact that a law school was found using quotas, something that violates anti-discrimination law and *Bakke*. Greve sympathizes "But no matter how elaborate the disguise, every school that strives for "diversity" will prohibit true competition among applicants across racial lines. The need to do so is dictated by the fundamental fact that drives the entire quota machinery: the dearth of qualified black (and, to a lesser extent, Hispanic) applicants."

Even the general four-fifths rule of bottom line adverse impact is only a general rule. There are certainly cases in which it is important. For example, in *EEOC v. Sears, Roebuck and Co.* (1986), the court rejected a prima facie case of disparate treatment because of lack of bottom line evidence. In *Hester v. Southern Railway Company* (1974), the court of appeals overturned a decision against the use of interviewing and testing, despite their subjective nature because the selection procedures had not resulted in adverse impact.

On the other hand, in *Connecticut v. Teal* (1982), the Supreme Court reviewed an interesting case. A test was given that many blacks failed, but for those who did pass, other selection components favored blacks over white so that the bottom line numbers were appropriate. Nevertheless, the Court said: "...Congress never intended to give an employer license to discriminate against some employees on the basis of race or sex merely because he favorably treats other members of the employees group." The problem in *Connecticut* seemed to be the fact that failing the one test was an absolute bar for some people to go further in the selection process. The majority opinion affirmed the circuit courts opinion that "where all of the candidates participate in the entire selection process, and the overall results reveal no significant disparity in impact, scrutinizing individual questions or individual sub-tests would, indeed, conflict with the dictates of common sense."

Staying Out of Court

General guidelines

Much of this section is drawn from Seymour (1988). If you're a psychologist, or a business person who plans to use tests, this attorney perspective on how to sue people who use cognitive tests will probably make you angry. It's a wise person who knows his/her adversary, however!

Don't wave a red flag

But do what's necessary. Courts have even upheld height requirements, *Blake v. Los Angeles* (1977), for example. In this case, the nature of the job, its high-potential impact, and the support for these claims made the requirement valid. Remember— first do what's right.

Good intentions

While Title VII cases did not, at one time, involve a jury, the Civil Rights Act of 1991 changed that. In addition, other employment law cases have allowed plaintiffs to ask for a jury (Arvey, 1988).

Sound test items

Scholars such as Gormly (1985) argue for the importance of sound individual test items. In *Soroka v. Dayton Hudson* (1991) (see Freiberg and DeAngelis, 1992), the plaintiff successfully argued that an employer has no right to ask invasive questions even when those items are empirically based and contribute to an overall score. Regardless of how this dispute is ultimately resolved, it reminds us that weird-sounding items are likely to be a problem. As Seymour (1988, p. 348) points out: "Just as tests and validation studies marked by obvious signs of common sense are less likely to be challenged, those marked by obvious lack of common sense are more likely to be challenged."

Chapter 9

The perfect alternative

Seymour, an attorney, derides the test products derived from the "soft data" of the social sciences as compared to the physical sciences (1988). One could argue that the data of social sciences are not simply soft opinions and that the experiments of the physical sciences are not as invariant and objective. (See comments about the physical science in notes for chapter 3). Perhaps Seymour has heard of the "cold fusion" debate since writing the article. But, putting defensiveness aside, comparing predictions concerning the speed of sound at sea level versus cognitive test validity generalization is admittedly an unequal fight. Nevertheless, Seymour does not hint at what might be better than a test at predicting behavior.

Of course, Seymour writes from the point of view of an attorney, and the attorney is not paid to find the best method of testing, but to win money for the plaintiff. But, nonattorneys (Goldstein & Patterson, 1988) sometimes take the same stance. Goldstein and Patterson are concerned about the discriminatory effects of cognitive tests, but make no mention of the court cases showing the interview and education requirements to be discriminatory.

Norton (1977) simply doesn't want discrimination, whether or not it is by valid means. But, if we are not going to have a basis for testing, we would either discriminate with no basis or have some sort of quota system.

Amazingly, people talk about "asking around," "having people write essays," and—incredibly—hold up the interview as a selection method. There is no perfect alternative, and the interview is generally a bad alternative.

The Interview

A strange story

Business owners should be concerned about theft, since the Commerce Department estimates 40 billion dollar business losses due to employee theft (see McCoy, 1989). A survey of CEOs showed that the vast majority was concerned about the effect of drug usage at the workplace in terms of increased medical benefit claims, decreased productivity, and many other areas. Business owners are also aware that they are responsible for the actions of their people. (See chapter 8 for a discussion of negligent hiring). Not surprisingly, business owners such as retailers are very interested in any test that can help screen out people who will steal or use drugs (see Ernst and Young, 1992).

Integrity tests have many problems. Nevertheless, Sackett and Harris (1984) found that they often predicted relevant criteria, and in an update (Sackett, Burris, & Callahan, 1989), the authors noted: "Thus a more compelling case that integrity tests predict a number of outcomes of interest to organizations can be made today than at the time of the earlier review." In the same review they point out: "Thus there is a large body of evidence indicating that women and racial minority groups are not adversely affected by either overt integrity tests or personality-oriented measures."

While integrity tests have problems, interviews have all the same problems and many more, as we will see. The Office of Technology Assessment (U.S. Congress, OTA, 1990) reviewed integrity tests and had many criticisms as well as many good suggestions. In comparing integrity tests to interviews, the report acknowledges "Alternative methods to screen out dishonest job applicants, such as subjective interviews or letters of reference, are also imperfect and can result in erroneous decisions." The report goes on to *defend* the interview in what may be one of the most singularly bizarre chains of reasoning encountered in a scholarly report. The reasoning is that since integrity tests are more reliable than interviews, interviews are "...less likely to be as consistently wrong as integrity tests about specific individuals." Using this reasoning, the OTA might also recommend the use of patent medicine over penicillin on the grounds that penicillin will consistently kill those with allergic reactions while patent medicine would more fairly kill people at random. For further information on honesty testing, read chapter 10 and chapter notes. The American Psychological Association (as quoted in BNA Employee Relations Weekly, March 18, 1991, p. 283) certainly sees the problems of integrity tests, but also says, "there is no sound basis for prohibiting their development and use; indeed, to do so would only invite alternative forms of pre-employment testing that would be less open, scientific and controllable." How nice to know that some people stop to evaluate alternatives.

The Facts About the Interview

The interview is a test

Read chapter 1 and if you find it hard to believe, get a copy of the Uniform Guidelines and read it for yourself. The interview (and anything else you do to select people) is a test.

But wait! Perhaps that's only in theory. Has anyone ever gone to court over the interview? In 1971, EEOC ruled that an employer's decision not to hire a black woman because of her "bad attitude" in the interview was a violation of Title VII (EEOC Decision No. 72-0703,4 FEP 435, 1971). In *King v. New Hampshire Department of Human Resources and Economic Development* (1977), the court ruled that questions in the interview had discriminatory intent because they were not relevant to the job. In *Weiner v. County of Oakland* (1976), the court found the interview wanting because of its subjective nature. In *Reynolds v. Sheet Metal Workers*, (1981), the circuit court ruled that subjective interviews were illegal when adverse impact resulted. In following sections you can also read about *United States v. Hazelwood School District* (1976) and *Presbyterian Hospital* (1989).

Interviewers jump to conclusions

In one study (Webster, 1964) it was found that most personnel interviewers made their decisions after 4 minutes of a 15-minute interview.

Interviewers dwell on negatives

Arvey (1979) cites studies that show that interviewers primarily search for reasons to reject job candidates.

Interviewers look at the wrong things

Interview judgments are often based on superficial characteristics unrelated to job success (Dipboye & Wiley, 1975). Yet, people think of themselves as being good at "sizing people up."

Let's take detection of people telling lies as an example. I visited with one Human Resources Director, who was also an attorney, who discussed validity data of testing at length followed by the casual assertion that he could tell a lot about integrity by watching how people shifted their eyes. He's probably not alone in thinking he can do that. What does the evidence show? Ekman and O'Sullivan (1991) reviewed several studies (e.g., DePaulo, Stone, & Lassiter, 1985; Kraut, 1980; Zuckerman, DePaulo, & Rosenthal, 1981) that showed that college students were not able to detect lying at above chance level. Researchers reasoned that college students had not been trained to detect lies and used experienced lie catchers. Kruat and Poe (1980) looked at customs inspectors, DePaulo and Pfeifer (1986) looked at federal law enforcement officers, and Kohnken (1987) examined police officers, and in all three studies, the "experts" did no better than college students. Ekman and O'Sullivan (1991) did a more sophisticated study in which there *were* lie-correlated behaviors in video-taped interviews, behavior that could be observed if people knew what to look for. The tapes were then observed by several groups of people, including college students, people taking a lie-detection course and some experts. On a 5-point scale of self-rated lie-detection ability, the experts rated themselves quite highly: psychiatrists only average (2.9), judges a bit above average (3.3), while federal polygraphers (3.6), robbery investigators (3.5), and Secret Service officers (3.8) rated themselves highly. These professionals would have good reason to rate themselves highly. How did they perform?

The Secret Service sample consistently scored above chance in lie detection. All other groups, including psychiatrists, judges, federal polygraphers, and robbery investigators, scored at chance level.

Yet, the popular literature flourishes with body language handbooks, and interviewers swap secrets about the meaning of shifty eyes. If judges and robbery investigators are unable to detect deceit, how much confidence do you have in your personnel officer?

Interviewers let stereotypes affect their judgment

Brehm and Kassin (1990, p. 148) discuss the *outgroup homogeneity* bias: "...a tendency to assume that there is greater similarity among members within outgroups than within ingroups. In other words, people are generally quite aware of the fine, sometimes subtle differences between individuals within their own groups. When it comes to outgroups, however, 'they' are all alike."

Stereotypes are often negative. In 1933, 75% of college students described blacks as lazy. This has improved across the years, but in 1967 there were still 26%

who held that stereotype (Karlines, Coffman, & Walters, 1969). Schein (1973) found that when male managers were asked to describe men in general, women in general and successful middle managers, the description of the successful middle manager was similar to the description of men. Men were predisposed to assume that a female candidate would not meet standards for successful midmanagement. Cecil, Paul, and Olins (1973) found that interviewers used different standards for evaluating men and women. Heilman, Martell, and Simon (1988) found that college students act to serve as interviewers (and some interviewers have no more experience than college students) tend to be gender biased in several different ways.

Gordon, Rozelle, and Baxter (1988) conducted an interesting study in which they showed that increasing accountability led to an increased bias against age. They hypothesized that interviewers under pressure might rely on easily accessible stereotypes. The limitation of the study was the use of student interviewers, but, realistically, some interviewers have no more sophistication than college students in the interview process.Other research has also shown that interviewers have age bias. (See Raza & Carpenter, 1987, who present their own evidence as well as researchers such as Avolio, 1982; and Haefner, 1977).

Stereotypes are used, and, sadly, stereotypes are often false. Arvey (1979), points out the many similarities in psychological variables across gender, race, and age. In a comparison of male and female managers matched by position type (Rose, 1992), managers were quite similar in terms of traits critical to management regardless of gender. This is simply a confirmation of what scholars like Bentz (1985) have demonstrated already.

Interviews are conducted by humans who have the biases of most humans. An objective test will treat men and women alike and will not be "pre-scored" on the basis of the race of the test taker.

Interviewers are subjective and inconsistent

As the court said of the interview process in *United States v. Hazelwood School District* (1976) "No evidence was presented which would indicate that any two principals apply the same criteria—objective or subjective—to evaluate applicants." Raza and Carpenter (1987) show that men and women interviewers conduct interviews differently. Gollub and Campion (1991) point out, in their review of court cases regarding the interview, that two factors are critical in court decisions—consistency and job relevance. These are two areas in which many interviews not only fall short, but fall terribly short.

Do you know what your interviewers are telling people?

In *King v. New Hampshire Department of Human Resources and Economic Development* (1977), interviewers asked a female applicant for the meter patrol if she could use a sledgehammer or "run somebody in." Since those questions had nothing to do with the job, they were used as evidence of discriminatory intent.

Arvey and Faley (1988) discuss a case involving EEOC and the New York Human Rights Commission in which they conclude that a law firm had been discriminatory by consistently emphasizing to women applicants that there were few women in the firm and they were assigned to roles different than men.

In *Presbyterian Hospital* (Labor Relations Reference Manual, 131, July 31, 1989, p. 180) an employer unlawfully eliminated a candidate from consideration because the interviewer asked the candidate questions about union sympathies.

If interviewers ask the wrong things—and who can be sure what they are asking—there can be serious problems.

The interview is usually a bad test

Hunter and Hunter (1984) review many different test procedures from cognitive tests to education requirements and find the validity of interviews to be quite low. While cognitive tests have the highest validity correlation coefficients at around .50, the interview is one of the weakest at .14. In other words, a test will account for 20 times more of the variance than most interviews. Based on the information we have discussed thus far, that is certainly to be expected. McDaniel, Whetzel, Schmidt, Hunter, Maurer, and Russell (1988) found a higher validity for the interview, but it was still lower than that for cognitive ability tests; hence the problems of bias and inconsistency still remain.

Edward Mitchell (1992), Partner in the Labor and Employment Law Department of the international law firm of Thompson, Hine, and Flory, speaks cogently to the issue of selection by interview. He wisely points out, "It is important to remember that EEOC's 'testing guidelines' apply to any employee selection procedure shown to have an adverse impact." He goes on to contrast standardized tests with the interview and states, "Subjective selection criteria such as the impressions of a supervisor formed during a thirty minute interview are far more difficult to defend. If procedures such as the interview result in disparate impact requiring validation, the employer is effectively dead in the water since there is virtually no way for any but the largest employers to statistically validate those subjective determinations."

The interview does have a place!

Guion (1991) points out that the interview has a public relations role and may assess some things, for example, conversational fluency, better than a test. He cites a number of studies (Arvey, Miller, Gould, & Burch, 1987; Ghiselli, 1966; Janz, 1982; Latham & Saari, 1984; Latham, Saari, Pursell, & Campion, 1980; McMurry, 1947; Orpen, 1985) that show that systematic and well-structured interviews are more effective than interviews that "just happen." Schmitt and Robertson's (1990) review also indicated that structured interviews could be effective and valid for some situations. The interview is not a substitute for a test, but it does have a place if done properly. Schmidt (1988) feels that the interview can substantially augment cognitive testing, for example.

Always remember that interviewers are affected by other information. The math test does not know what you put on your application blank—the interviewer does, and it affects his/her decision making (see Dipboye and Phillips, 1989). Is this bias or integration of information good or bad? It can be both. Make sure your interviewers have good information (application blanks, etc) because they will be affected by it.

Other Alternatives

Assessment centers

Guion (1991, pp. 350, 365) discusses the value of assessment centers for managerial selection and discusses research that supports the value of this approach. The main limitation of the assessment center is that while it may be feasible for high-level positions, it is probably not feasible for hiring at all levels.

Evaluation of experience and education

Arvey (1979) points out that "Case law has progressed to the point where it is fairly clear that educational requirements will not survive challenge given adverse impact and the absence of validity evidence." He mentions specific cases, including *Johnson v. Goodyear Tire and Rubber Co.* (1974) in which a high school diploma requirement was disallowed. In another case, *Pettway v. American Cast Iron Pipe Co.* (1974), the court reviewed a case in which a high school diploma was required for admission into an apprenticeship program. The court did not disagree with the contention that reading and study skills were important for the apprenticeship, but said, "Many high school courses needed for a diploma (history, literature, physical education, etc.) are not necessary for these abilities...a high school diploma or equivalent criterion does not effectively measure the reading and study skills necessary for the course work required by the apprenticeship." Education and experience requirements may be justified in some cases—but they must be justified. Read McDaniel and Schmidt (1985) which can be found in a good academic library, for a discussion of the best ways to evaluate experience and training.

Reference checks

Norton (1977) objects to the use of any test, validated or not, because they will discriminate against blacks. But, anything can! As one alternative, Norton suggests "calling around" about job candidates—as if a reference check is going to be consistent and fair! As Arvey and Faley (1988, p. 301) point out, "In terms of validity, the published research on the reference check is not particularly encouraging."

Why not use them all?

For example, studies have shown that cognitive tests improve the validity of assessment centers (Thornton & Byham, 1982). Cognitive tests combined with personality tests improve job performance predictions (Day & Silverman, 1989). Schmidt (1988) estimates that cognitive ability tests can improve the validity of the interview correlation by .15.

Chapter 10

Misplaced Concerns and False Arguments

Minorities never do well on tests

In fact, in the often-maligned integrity tests, blacks perform no differently than whites (see Sackett, Burris, & Callahan, 1989). In some personality test studies, black high school students were more outgoing and socially dominant (key factors for management success) than their white counterparts (see Johnson & Cottle, 1952). There are many types of tests and not all discriminate.

Tests are not valid, consistent, fair...compared to...?

See chapter 9. Whenever testing is challenged, there should be two sides to the exchange: support for the test; support for the "unknown but better alternative." Otherwise we have the logical error that Fearnside and Holther (1959, p. 66) refer to as "Logic-Chopping." "It is a form of perfectionism to reject the best available on the grounds that it is not the best conceivable. What is happening seems to be a rejection of serviceable usages for the sole reason that there are cases that are marginal or doubtful."

Most hassles are with hiring!

Before any hiring action, recruiting can be a legal hassle. In *EEOC v. Detroit Edison* (1975) the practice of relying on referrals by a predominantly white workforce was ruled discriminatory.

After you have hired, promotion and discharge decisions can lead to even more liability. In addition to *Rowe v. General Motors* (1972), consider *Wade v. Mississippi Cooperative Extension Service* (1974), *Statsny v. Southern Bell Telephone and Telegraph Co.* (1978), and *EEOC v. Sandia Corp.* (1980). What do all of these cases have in common? First, they are about promotion, not hiring, and second, they do not involve objective standardized testing, they involve subjective appraisals. *Brito v. Zia* (1973) involved layoff decisions—not hiring—based on a performance evaluation form, not a test. Lublin (1991) writing for the *Wall Street Journal* points out: "But comparatively few people complain about allegedly unfair hiring these days. Nearly 61% of the bias charges filed with the Equal Employment Opportunity Commission in fiscal 1990 targeted advancement and discharge decisions. Only 8.6% aimed at hiring." Also, see the sections on negligent hiring.

Tests are flawed and legally liable. The interview is a better alternative!

Over a decade ago, I wrote a very short article, which, I feared, merely pointed out the obvious—that every selection device, including the interview was a test (1980). I simply *quoted* from the Uniform Guidelines (1978)! Yet, even today, people continue to see the interview as a safe alternative—so perhaps stating (and re-stating) the obvious is necessary! Read chapter 9 before you make the mistake of using the interview as a "safe alternative" to the test." As chapter 8 points out, you can't "play it safe"—and relying on the interview alone is definitely "playing it dumb."

The better alternative

There is absolutely no support whatsoever for the interview, the reference check, experience, education, or any of the other commonly (casually) touted alternatives. As replacements for tests they have all of the problems and none of the advantages. If anyone mentions one of these better alternatives, please ask him/her for the evidence to support it.

Tests don't work!

Modern tests are incredibly powerful. Let's look at the two major sets of tests: cognitive and personality.

Cognitive Tests

At one time, people made the seemingly logical contention that "intelligence" was a general concept, not as important in predicting job success as more directly related "competency" traits. McClelland (1973) argued that intelligence tests were like games, games that did not predict practical success. Barret and Depinet (1991) compared McClelland's claims against actual research and found that intellectual tests *do* predict later job success.

Schmidt (1988) convincingly shows that cognitive tests are valid predictors for performance in a wide range of jobs. Cognitive tests predict job success better than grades, educational background, reference checks, or interviews (Hunter & Hunter, 1984). Also see Schmidt and Hunter (1981) and Zedeck and Cascio (1984). Gutenberg, Arvey, Osburn, and Jeanneret (1983) indicated that cognitive tests are valid over a wide range of occupations: "A variety of studies have demonstrated that even fairly gross task and job differences do not appear to moderate validities in the manner previously believed."

Nor is there one specific test that is magic. We have known for years (see Spearman, 1904, 1927) that there is a g factor that underlies many different types of cognitive tests and scholastic grades. This is reflected in the high intercorrelations of all types of cognitive ability tests. The Watson-Glaser Critical Thinking Appraisal (1980), a test of general reasoning, correlates significantly with the Scholastic Aptitude Tests (Math and Verbal), the WAIS, and others tests. A 5-minute test of vocabulary (the EAS-1, see Ruch & Ruch, 1963) correlates .75 with the Verbal portion of the SCAT. Any testing textbook will supply you with as many correlations as you wish to examine. Also, see Thorndike (1986) for a discussion of the importance of the g factor.

We have discussed the concept of "validity generalization," a concept courts have supported. In *Friend v. Leidinger* (1977), the court said: "To require local validation in every city, village and hamlet would be ludicrous." This was again affirmed in *Pegues v. Mississippi State Employment Service* (1980) in which the court said: "Plaintiff's allegation that validity is specific to a particular location, a particular set of tasks and to a specific applicant population or in other words, that a valid test in one set of circumstances is not valid in circumstances not perfectly identical is not true." Thus, the courts have reaffirmed that validity can generalize when tasks are similar; proponents of the utility of g maintain that almost all job tasks have in common the need for general intelligence. The Industrial and Organizational Society Principles (1987) affirm: "Current research has shown that the differential effects of numerous variables are not so great as heretofore assumed; much can be attributed to statistical artifacts...It now seems well established from both validity generalization studies and cooperative validation efforts that validities generalize far more than once supposed" (Society for I/O, 1987, p. 26).

But not everyone agrees with validity generalization of cognitive tests. Goldstein and Patterson (1988), writing in a special issue of *Journal of Vocational Behavior* dealing with the g factor in employment, indicated in very emotional terms, that validity generalization was simply another attempt at racial discrimination. Seymour (1988), an attorney writing in that same issue, argued that validity generalization is not cogent in the soft social sciences.

Nevertheless, the majority of psychologists writing in that special issue concurred with Gordon, Lewis, and Quigley (1988) that Seymour's statistical argument was "...wrong and seriously misleading." As Levin (1988) concludes: "There is probably some relation between general ability and job performance for most jobs...At the very least there is likely to be an ability threshold that is necessary to perform a job..."

Concurrent validation studies work well with cognitive tests, that is, there is nothing about the job that alters intelligence, so testing of incumbents may generalize to new hires. (See Guion's 1991 review of studies such as Schmitt, Gooding, Noe, & Kirsch, 1984.) Schmidt, Hunter, Outerbridge, and Goff (1988) demonstrated that cognitive ability difference does not disappear with time and experience even after 5 years.

It is only when we step from research and statistics and look at the world with some common sense that the power of cognitive tests becomes less surprising than obvious. The world has long known that it is important to be able to read, write, reason, and perform basic math.

Certainly, intelligence is important in professional positions. CPAs, physicians, psychologists, lawyers, and other professionals have to take exams in school, and for their state boards, tests that involve a good deal of verbal intelligence. In management, the importance of intelligence is shown time and again. In his review of hundreds of studies concerning management traits, Stodgill (1974) lists intelligence as a key trait.

Intelligence does not apply only to "professional" jobs. Almost all jobs have obvious intelligence factors in the very content. The carpenter must know that cutting $5/8$ inch off a $10\frac{1}{2}$-inch board will result in a $9\frac{7}{8}$-inch board—is it surprising that math has something to do with the job? The waiter must be able to remember which orders will be done first to insure getting out the proper orders—he has to remember and reason. Like many other attributes of human beings, for example, weight, physical strength, personality, and intelligence can be enhanced but it is difficult to do. See Gottfredson's discussion (1988, p. 298).

Let's say it one last time in simple words: There is nothing magical about cognitive tests, as a review of their contents will almost always show. They measure vocabulary, reasoning, and math. Our world involves the ability to reason, read, communicate, and use math. That's why all civilizations in Africa, America, Europe, and China have taught the 3 Rs. And as for "culture fair" tests, read about them in the following sections.

Personality Inventories

In the 1960s psychologists had serious questions about the ability of personality tests to predict work performance. Since the business world has long-held the importance of personal attributes to be key to success, the attitude of psychologists is a bit odd. Perhaps they felt themselves to be more scientifically correct than dull-witted business professionals. Plain old common sense would suggest that personality factors involving attitude toward life and orientation to deal with people would have an effect on the many jobs that involve dealing with people. Time proved (once again) that common sense and the "dull" business leaders were right.

Ghiselli (1973) reviewed validity studies and found that while validities are unimpressive for clerical occupations, they are encouraging for sales and managerial jobs. In 1991, Guion said that his earlier review (Guion & Gottier, 1965) commonly read as saying personality tests did not have a use in selection was simply misinterpreted. Guion does caution that personality traits may be molded by the environment. For example, perhaps it's not that confidence helps make a good salesperson; perhaps salespeople are self-confident because success has made them so. Guion assumes a lot of malleability in an adult personality! If Guion's reasoning were correct, basing claims on concurrent validation studies would not afford much future prediction. But, again, the common sense notion that personality tends to become stable is borne out by research. Costa of the National Institute of Aging (cited in Adler, 1992) affirms the common sense notion that while personality can change, it tends to "set in plaster by age 30." Five-factor tests *do* have good future prediction, especially after enough time has passed on the job for the "honeymoon effect"—that is, that initial period in which the employee is working hard to make a good impression—to pass (Helmreich, Sawin, & Carsrud, 1986). Hogan (1991) reviews a number of studies showing that good five-factor inventories such as the Guilford-Zimmerman Temperament Survey can predict a variety of job success criteria decades into the future. Harrell and Harrell (1984) and Sparks (1983) are good examples of the studies reviewed.

In short, personality is relatively stable (the introverts today will probably be introverts next week), and personality variables as measured by tests predict job success. Work interests are closely related to personality and show a great deal of stability across time (see Holland, 1985, especially discussion of stability, p. 128).

Summing it up for Cognitive Ability and Personality

If anything, the true power of tests is often underestimated due to poor criteria. Schmitt, Gooding, Noe, and Kirsch (1984) examined 350 validity studies and found that more objective criteria, such as status change or earnings, show higher validities than supervisor ratings. Meyer (1987) found that test validities, which were slight and nonsignificant for predicting one-time performance ratings, become large and significant when performance over time or salary progression is used as criteria. Harrell and his colleagues (Harrell, 1969, 1970, 1972; Harrell & Harrell,1973, 1984) use real-life criteria such as earnings after graduation and find strong relationships between personality factors and management success.

In an 8-year assessment center study at AT&T, Bray Campbell and Grant (1974) found the strongest predictor of management success was "Oral Communication Skill" followed closely by "Human Relations Skill." Kotter (1982) observed effective managers and found that they worked long hours and spent a great deal of time in persuasive personal interaction with their subordinates. Yukl and Van Fleet (1992), in reviewing decades of research, conclude that leadership is characterized by such things as high energy, integrity, emotional maturity, stress tolerance, self-confidence, interpersonal skills, and conceptual skills such as analytical ability.

In other words, people in management must have certain personality traits (e.g., human relations skill, energy, self-confidence, and stress tolerance) and certain cognitive abilities (e.g., communication skill and conceptual skill). They must have these traits to be able to formulate their thoughts, deal with people and match the fast pace of business. Tests that measure those abilities will predict success. Wouldn't you be surprised at any other result?

Employers are Dropping the Use of Testing!

Let's look at a 1992 survey, reported in *Human Resource Executive* (1992). Based on a survey of 497 human resource executives:

- About 30% expect pre-employment and developmental testing to increase, 60% to stay the same. Those few who did foresee a reduction in use did so because of recession-linked budget issues.
- Highest priorities to lowest, top down:
  - Skills testing
  - Drug and integrity testing
  - Personality/psychology testing
  - Physical testing
  - Assessment center/workplace simulations
  - General aptitude tests
  - Background checks

Honesty Testing

Honesty testing was contrasted with the interview in chapter 9, so some of the following discussion may seem familiar. Let's review the case for honesty or integrity testing. Sackett and Harris (1984) (updated 1989 by Sackett, Burris, & Callahan) examined a number of honesty tests, dealing with theft, drug usage, and so forth. Since test items include not only empirically validated items, but often admissions, it is not surprising that, in general, honesty tests correlate well with various criteria.

It is also comforting for test users that no biases are found on the basis of race or gender. From a psychometric and EEOC point of view, honesty tests look good.

From the point of view of the employer, honesty testing is important. Business loses about $40 billion per year to theft in the workplace (see Gazner, 1990). The U.S. Chamber of Commerce estimates 75% of employees steal at least once, and half are repeat offenders (McCoy, 1989). The National Institute on Drug Abuse, in a 1988 study, indicated that among persons 26-34, 13% of those employed had used illegal drugs within the last month and over 24% of those not employed had done so (see Drexler, 1990).

The consumer pays much of this price, of course. The U.S. Department of Commerce says thieves and programs to catch them add up to 15% of the price of every item purchased (McCoy, 1989).

Business leaders must do something to stem this tide. In their survey of retail loss prevention, Ernst and Young (1992) found that 47% of the respondents were using honesty testing.

What about the point of view of the test taker? Is it fair to require such tests? Arnold (1992) cites the opinion of the American Psychological Association that research shows people seldom object to taking tests when the relevance is clear and the items are straightforward. (In the *Soroka* case, by contrast, the objection was to indirect and invasive items whose content was not directly related to the specific job). From the point of view of neither the employer nor the employee, but the general public, de Bernardo (of the Institute for a Drug-free Workplace) says

"Employers have a duty to provide an environment safe for workers and customers."

Lewis Maltby, National Director of the American Civil Liberties Union's Task Force on the Workplace sums the situation up best: "The employer has a legitimate concern about hiring honest, drug-free employees. The worker has a legitimate concern that his privacy be respected and that he has equal opportunity, free of discrimination. Differences arise over what tool is used." (Maltby and de Bernardo are quoted in Gazner's 1990 Parade article.)

You will hear *very* vocal and often heated opinions from both sides of the honesty testing issue. Some proponents are, of course, people who sell honesty tests. Thus they are hardly unbiased. Who is unbiased? Politicians who want votes? Academics who have never worked in a for-profit environment?

If you look at the two sides of the issue, you will see three common trends in the debate: business experience versus no business experience, academic versus practical, and invasion versus utility.

Let's look at the issue of business experience. People who have little experience in making business profitable advocate doing away with testing in favor of other devices. For example, in BNA's *Employee Relations Weekly*, March 18, 1991, Tiner, former Director of Government Affairs for the United Food and Commercial Workers Union made suggestions concerning alternatives to testing. These alternatives included: reference checks, background checks, and interviews. Strayer, Director of Government relations for the National Association of Convenience Stores, countered by "blasting" the interview as the most biased and discriminatory way to hire, citing cases where "broccoli in the teeth" leads to rejection of an applicant.

A second trend: People who point out flaws in honesty testing without pointing to a viable alternative versus those who point out the potential savings in using even a flawed tool. In BNA's *Employee Relations Weekly*, March 18, 1991, psychologist Tenopyr points out the many problems associated with integrity tests. In the same article, Human Resources Director Pardue points out that a 3-year test use of an honesty test reduced shrinkage by 50% at a savings of $1.25 million. So, is it a flawed tool or the best alternative? *Yes* to both!

With regard to these first two debates, research (not to mention common sense) certainly supports the idea that it's better to do some good with an imperfect tool than to do less good or even harm with an even more imperfect tool. Let the American Psychological Association (APA) sum it up. The APA (as quoted in BNA's *Employee Relations Weekly*, March 18, 1991, p. 283) certainly sees the problems of integrity tests but also says, "there is no sound basis for prohibiting their development and use; indeed, to do so would only invite alternative forms of pre-employment testing that would be less open, scientific and controllable."

The third debate issue is a bit more serious. In BNA's *Employee Relations Weekly*, June 11, 1990, Attorney Seligman is cited as arguing that honesty tests invade privacy; Attorney Birenbaum argues that tests are valuable for business. Value for business is important—but so is individual privacy! Be sure to read the discussion of privacy. We must balance the rights of the individual job applicant with the public he/she may affect.

It's fifty-fifty, so it's chance level

Chance level is .50 only when you have *two equally likely alternatives*. A probability of .50 can be extremely high. Don't let anyone make the analogy of flipping a coin unless that is really the case. The chance of getting a "royal flush/or not" is *not* two equally likely alternatives.

You've never actually shown

By analogy, we might imagine an attorney saying, "Detective Smith, have you ever shown that this revolver with this bullet would have killed Mr. Jones, that individual, if shot?"

"No," the detective stammers, "but it seems..."

"Aha! You haven't shown that this revolver with this bullet would injure this man!"

Many people are unaware of the fact that *all* sciences, not just the social sciences, are *not* based on facts like links in a chain, but "...a web drawn together at certain points. The web endures as a whole, the strength of each strand contributing to the strength of the others" (Fearnside & Holther, 1959, p. 6). How did scientists know so much about the planets long before actually sending landing craft? By making generalizations based on a web of facts. There are many cases in which you may be using selection techniques that have not been proven with that test with that group; you will have to use construct validity, that is, build a logical argument for what you are doing, and you will have to make generalizations about your tests.

As discussed in the section on cognitive tests, tests of intelligence generalize well to many different situations. The National Research Council of the National

Academy of Science (Wigdor & Garner, 1982) states: "We find little convincing evidence that well-constructed and competently administered tests are more valid predictors for one subgroup than another: individuals with higher scores tend to perform better on the job, regardless of group identity."

Hogan (1991) reviews studies by many researchers covering many different studies of managerial effectiveness and finds consistent predictions across many situations and criteria. From the point of view of psychological testing, interest testing, and business knowledge (see Yukl, 1981) people in enterprising positions (see Holland, 1985) must be energetic and socially dominant.

There are aspects of jobs and related abilities that can be generalized. And, fortunately, the courts show remarkable common sense in recognizing that test measurements can be generalized. *Pegues v. Mississippi State Employment Service* (1980): "Plaintiffs allegation that validity is specific to a particular location, a particular set of tasks and to a specific applicant population or in other words, that a valid test in one set of circumstances is not valid in circumstances not perfectly identical is not true." *Friend v. Leidinger* (1977): "To require local validation in every city, village and hamlet would be ludicrous."

It is scientifically reasonable to make generalizations when based on good reasoning and is, in fact, the rule more than the exception.

The Government needs to protect people from tests!

Allen (1988) of the U. S. Commission on Civil Rights gives a wonderful example of what happens when the government protects people by focusing on methods rather than intent and effect. In the state of California a federal court ruling has said that no black child may be given an IQ test. Mary Amaya's son had been assigned—based on a subjective evaluation—for remedial courses. Mrs. Amaya had encountered that sort of racial bias before, with an older son. At that time she used the results of an IQ test to refute that misclassification. She was unable to do that for her younger son because the new ruling "protected" him! As Allen says: "Where objective measures in the past had vouchsafed occasion for individuals to vindicate themselves, today subjective measures have been forced to the forefront, restored to the role they played in the discrimination against my father." Recently (see Turkington, 1992) a U.S. District Judge changed his earlier ruling in *Larry P. v. Riles* (1979) to allow black children to be tested under some circumstances. What long-term effects this ruling will have are yet to be seen.

Of course you say that, you're biased

Consider the remarks of Norton (1977, cited in Sharf, 1988) then Chair of EEOC. Norton speaks out openly against testing, not because tests are invalid but because they discriminate. "There is not any way in which black people tomorrow as a group are going to, no matter what kind of test you give them, score the same way that white people score...I can't live with that. I think employers can. And I think test validation gives them an A-1 out." Norton has a bias: she wants to see black people get jobs. Her statement certainly doesn't give the impression that she's hardly searching for psychometric validity—nor, perhaps should that be expected.

See Fernside and Holther for a discussion of the "fallacy of origin" (1959, p. 97). As usual, the authors bring cold logic to heated disputes; for example, "The fact that the plan is backed by a source whose strong economic interest provides an obvious reason for anticipating bias does not justify dismissing the proposal without enquiry into its merits." Let's look at the *basis* not the *bias*.

You're wrong, so I'm right

Goldstein and Patterson (1988) attack the validity claims of other scholars (e.g., Gottfredson, 1988; Schmidt, 1988; Sharf, 1988) because over-use of such tests would lead to resegregation. In fact, cognitive tests might be quite valid *and* their over-use might lead to resegregation. Let's don't take a "you're wrong so I'm right" point of view! Read the suggestions in chapter 11.

Tests Discriminate—The Use of "Culture Fair" Tests

For most personality traits, Arvey and Faley (1988) show that there is high similarity between males and females, white and black, old and young. And personality factors are often quite important, especially in the business world of management and sales. See the section on "tests don't work."

See the research cited in chapter 9 and its chapter notes about the similarity in successful male and female managers, in addition to studies such as that of Howard and Bray (1988).

Carter and Swanson (1990) found that blacks showed a greater interest in business, sales occupations, and verbal-linguistic fields while whites showed a relatively stronger interest sciences and technical areas. To understand the importance of sales and management in the business world you must understand that sales is much more likely to lead to professional career advancement than technical skill (See Korn, 1988 for one example—or read any other business publications and problems of technical people who envy managerial and sales salaries!)

Johnson and Cottle (1952) found that black high school students scored higher than whites on the extraversion traits of ascendance and sociability—traits that have been shown to be strongly related to management success (see Hogan, 1991).

Howard and Bray (1988) showed that assessment center data demonstrate that blacks often have superior interpersonal skills and stability of performance.

There *is* variation in cognitive tests as a function of race. And tests are *very* effective, as discussed in the notes on "tests don't work." Are there "culture fair" alternatives?

Williams (1975) developed the BITCH (Black Intelligence Test of Cultural Homogeneity) in which he showed that terms such as "boogie jungle" and "alley apple" would be understood easily by blacks but not whites. His point about avoiding culturally laden items in tests is well taken, but the BITCH does not correlate well with more traditional measures of intelligence. Scholars also considered that perhaps tests with less verbal information and more emphasis on abstract reasoning would work. Arvey (1972) did a review showing that culture fair tests did not seem to work. More dramatically, Moore, MacNaughton, and Osborn (1969), Tenopyr (1967), and Higgins and Silvers (1958) indicated that disadvantaged groups actually perform *worse* on the so-called culture fair tests than on traditional tests. Campbell, Pike, Flaugher, and Mahoney, (1970) found job-related validities for blacks were higher for traditional tests than for nonverbal tests.

Many brave people, none braver than Dr. King (see King, 1992), fought for educational rights because they recognized the profound influence of education and the deficiency that African-Americans experienced in that area. There are long-term solutions to the problem but they don't exist in denial or in the search for some double standard. "We cannot aim merely to be good Negro teachers, good Negro doctors, or good Negro skilled laborers. We must set out to do a good job regardless of race" (King, p. 71).

Greve (1992) discusses the fact that a law school was found using quotas, something that violates antidiscrimination laws and the Supreme Court *Bakke v. Regents of the University of California* (1978). Greve sympathizes "But no matter how elaborate the disguise, every school that strives for "diversity" will prohibit true competition among applicants across racial lines. The need to do so is dictated by the fundamental fact that drives the entire quota machinery: the dearth of qualified black (and, to a lesser extent, Hispanic) applicants." This is not a disparaging remark about African-Americans. It is an indictment of society's failure to provide good education. It's a hot debate: *g* proponents point out that it is hard to change basic intelligence with training and that any testing that moves away from *g* will be decreasing validity. Despite previous research, some researchers (e.g., Helms, 1992) are still concerned about cultural bias in tests. People concerned with the effect this will have on hiring of African-Americans do not want to see *g* and associated cognitive testing overemphasized. Read all of the articles in the 1988 *Journal of Vocational Behavior Issue* to get a handle on the arguments.

Faking

Hogan (1991) reviews a number of studies that show that while people can fake, in practice they rarely do. Of more importance, many studies indicate that ability to fake is a sign of good adjustment. For example, Canter (1963, p. 905): "...there is a positive relationship between the ability to present a good picture on the CPI and actual life adjustment of the subject." Hogan summarizes the faking issue: "There is a large and replicated literature showing that well-adjusted people have positively biased self-images...Consequently, when one controls for self-deception, measures related to well-being and adjustment lose some of their predictive power."

Chapter 11

Future of Testing

Any technological advances will be of concern to some people. The computerized trend is a good example. How have computers affected testing? Computerized testing is faster (e.g., Wise & Plake, 1989). Even grade school children have no difficulty with computerized testing (Olson, Maynes, Slawson, & Ho, 1989), and some high school students actually perform better than on paper and pencil tests (Chin, Donn, & Conry, 1991). College students do as well with computerized testing and prefer it (Luken, Dowd, Plake, & Kraft, 1985). Davis and Cowles (1989) found computerized testing more reliable and less anxiety provoking than paper and pencil testing. They had some concern that the low anxiety might be related to faking, but other studies (Evan & Miller, 1969) have shown more honesty and candor in computerized testing.

Guion (1991) discusses the concerns that people had about computerized testing and sums it up well: "Yet, in a sense, they [computers] only permitted people to do better and faster what they had already been doing."

Item Response Theory

- Read about this new and powerful development in Drasgow and Hulin (1991).
- IRT looks at relationship of individual item to overall ability.
- IRT can look at the different incorrect responses and give partial credit (e.g., wrong answer a may be better than wrong answer b).

- Uses
  - To detect aberrant profiles: faking bad, cheating, and so forth.
  - To develop tests so that redundant items or items that are too easy are removed.
  - To develop tests so that no group (e.g., racial) bias is in test alternatives.
  - In the form of Computerized Adaptive Testing, the computer calculates based on each item and does not give unnecessarily hard or easy items—test is shortened because unnecessary items are eliminated. Testing is different for each person.

Suggestions

Gottfredson (1988) points out that g (general intelligence) is not strongly affected by training. Schmidt (1988) points out that skills tests are effective primarily because of g and that attempts to avoid discrimination by specific skills testing defeats the purpose of selection. He also points out that cut scores are not effective because success is linearly related to performance.

Nevertheless, in my opinion we *must* compromise, even if Gottfredson and Schmidt are completely correct. We simply can't ask African–Americans to wait a few generations while the effects of discrimination "wear off." Yes, intelligence may be important, but knowing specific job-related skills is content valid and trainable. In addition, Gottfredson (1988) points out that while training effects on intelligence are often negligible, there are some positive findings as well. Even general abilities such as logical reasoning can be improved by training (e.g., Sorenson, 1966).

The use of personality measures is vital, because they are important, certainly in management jobs (see Hogan, 1991). As an example, Howard and Bray (1988) showed that in high-potential managers, blacks scored lower than whites on cognitive tests but compensated with superior interpersonal skills and other personality factors.

APPENDIX

Doing Research in Testing

You may want to verify things for yourself!

Testing

Annual Review of Psychology. These annual reviews often contain sections about testing, selection and other relevant issues. See Schmidt, Ones, and Hunter (1992).

APA Standards. These standards are the American Psychological Association guidelines on the proper use of tests. In some cases they may have legal force like the Uniform Guidelines, even though they differ from the Uniform Guidelines in some areas.

APA I/O Standards. Very similar to those of the APA but written from the point of view of professionals in the Industrial and Organizational Psychology area.

Buros Mental Measurements Yearbook. Many tests are described in this yearbook along with articles written about the tests. The tests are frequently reviewed by scholars in the field. If you want to know more about a standard test, this is a good place to start. You should be able to find it in any library.

Computerized Literature Searches. Most university libraries will have data bases that you can search on the basis of authors, topics or titles. Make sure you know the scope of the data base, for example, psychological journals only or a data base that includes popular press and business. Also note the time scale, how far into the past the search extends, and how current the data base is.

Fallacy, the Counterfeit of Argument, Fearnside and Holther. Much of the use of testing is a matter of logical analysis and a review of any testing debate shows that to be in short supply! Arm yourself with good thinking habits. If you can't find *Fallacy* almost any book of logic will do. This one is the best.

Getting to Yes. Fisher and Ury show you how to defuse emotions and get people focused on the underlying issues rather than stated (and emotionally held) positions. Very few people are really "anti-testing"—many people have specific issues, for example, they are anti-invasion. The issue is how to minimize invasion, and, properly done, testing can *help*.

Handbook of Industrial and Organizational Psychology, 1990/1991/1992. The Handbook is published periodically, this being the latest version. There are articles not only on testing but on virtually all aspects of Industrial Psychology. Be sure to pay special attention to articles by Guion, Campbell, and Hogan.

Journal of Vocational Behavior, December 1988. The entire issue of this journal is devoted to discussion of the use of cognitive tests and contains pros and cons from top researchers in the field.

Making Vocational Choices. John Holland is one of the fathers of modern vocational theory. Holland is not only the creator of interest tests; the theory underlying his tests links personality, tests, and interests.

Psychological Abstracts. A brief abstract of psychology articles published in a number of psychological journals. The abstracts go back for years.

Psychological/Educational Journals. They can seem impenetrable, but don't despair. The first section is the *Introduction* in which the purpose of the article is discussed in light of previous research. The second section, *Method,* tells how the experiment was actually performed and who it was performed on (the subjects). The third section called *Results* is the one that tells you what actually happened. The last section is *Discussion,* and, being the author's opinion, may go off into the clouds.

Not all journals are created equal. The *Journal of Vocational Behavior* and any journal published by the American Psychological Association, especially the APA's *Journal of Applied Psychology*, are top notch. Check those that are "vanity press" (e.g., pay to print)—their standards may not be as tough as the journals listed above.

Psychological Testing, Anastasi. This covers the basic concepts of testing in detail. Information about specific tests will be out of date in many cases. Even in more recent versions of general testing books—including this one—don't rely on them for information about *specific tests.*

Scientific Citation Abstracts. This will tell you how often and by whom an article is cited. This tells you who is reading the articles.

Tests in Print. This book describes many tests, including some less-technical tests. It does not review the tests, but describes them and gives information on ordering the tests. You should be able to find this in the library.

Test Manuals for Particular Tests. Most tests have a manual of instructions and supporting information. In some cases you must be a licensed psychologist to obtain this information. You can contact test publishers and get their catalog and requirements for different types of tests. These are a few; you can find more in *Tests in Print.*

American Psychological Association
1-800-374-2721
P.O. Box 2710
Hyattsville, MD 20784-0710

Consulting Psychologists Press
1-800-624-1765
3803 E. Bayshore Road
Palo Alto, CA 94303

Institute for Personality and Ability Testing
1-800-225-4728
P.O. Box 1188
Champaign, IL, 61824-1188

Psychological Assessment Resources
1-800-331-TEST
P.O. Box 998
Odessa, FL 33556-9901

Legal Resources

BNA Employee Relations Weekly. These publications are a good way of keeping up with what's happening in terms of legal issues relating to testing. See also *Fair Employment Practices*. You may need to look specifically in a law school library.

Fair Employment Practices. Case law regarding employment cases, updated biweekly. See BNA *Employee Relations Weekly*.

Fairness in Selecting Employees. Many of the court cases discussed in this book were drawn from Arvey's work; the first edition was published in 1979, the second edition was published in 1988. It's a good all-around resource for the legal aspects of testing.

The Uniform Guidelines/ADA information. Write or call your local EEOC office for ADA information, Uniform Guidelines information, and so forth. Arvey's 1988 and 1979 *Fairness* book have the Uniform Guidelines reprinted in the back of the book.

Statistics

If you want to know more about statistics, read Hayes (1973). If you're ever faced with *meta-analysis*, don't faint. The statistics are sophisticated but the basic idea is pooling data from many separate and small studies, using statistical corrections. See Schmidt, Hunter, Pearlman, and Hirsh (1985).

Professionals You Can Consult

Psychologists are the main experts on tests. There are many types of psychologists. Experimental psychologists may know little or nothing about testing. Social psychologists may know a bit more. Educational psychologists may be familiar with tests primarily in the educational setting. Clinical psychologists may deal with tests such as Rorschach and MMPI, which are primarily clinical. Industrial psychologists are usually the ones who will know the most about industrial testing.

Labor and employment law attorneys can help you with legal concerns. Don't get trapped into the "don't do anything" recommendation because, legally speaking, doing nothing is doing something—you can't avoid risk; you want to know your best alternatives.

In an organization, your Human Resources Director may be a good source of information. Since these people are not licensed by any board, you will get a wide variation in test use sophistication. If, for example, a Human Resources Director thinks an interview is not a test, it means that he/she is not going to be a good source of information.

If Your Testing is in a Business Environment

You may be doing testing for government agencies, nonprofit organizations, and so forth. But if you're doing it within a business context, it might be a good idea to know something about business. How can you test for management skill if you don't know what that means?

Harvard Business Review. This premiere business journal contains some good ideas about managers, job demands, and other factors that are relevant to work.

Management of Organizational Behavior. One of the most common concerns in testing, especially at the salaried level, is the extent to which a person has leadership capabilities, where his/her capabilities best fit, and how these abilities can be developed. This book, by Hersey and Blanchard (1982) discusses a model of leadership that has been around for some time. It is popular, but often criticized (see Schein, 1980, p. 131) for not having clearly defined constructs. Nevertheless, as Schein illustrates, there are many similarities across a wide range of leadership models. The Hersey-Blanchard model is understandable and practical.

Search for Excellence. The whole "excellence" concept has degenerated to a buzzword, and Tom Peters has become more preacher than scholar. *Search*, however, was a well-researched book that points out that successful businesses have definite similarities, for example, a bias for action and a focus on customer service.

The Success Profile. Lester Korn, one-time Chairman of the search firm of Korn Ferry, tells about success traits in executives (e.g., intelligence, energy, likability) and the routes to success in management (sales, yes; personnel, unlikely).

These will get you started in the right section of the bookstore or library. It is interesting to view the business versus more traditional academic fields. After years of debate about leadership traits (including an interesting period in which some people said there were no such traits) psychology has discovered that people who are energetic, outgoing, intelligent, and honest tend to succeed in practically any job—especially management—to a far greater extent than those lacking these qualities. And those success traits apply regardless of age or gender. Guess what? Those dumb business professionals have known that for a long time.

Organizations of Interest

These organizations may be helpful in providing information about the use of testing in business.

American Society of Training Directors
American Psychological Association
Society for Industrial and Organizational Psychology
Society for Human Resource Management

Legal Case References

Albemarle v. Moody, 10 FEP 1181 (1975).

Allen v Alabama State Board of Education, No. 81-697-N (1985).

Blake v. the City of Los Angeles, 15 FEP 77 (1977).

Brito v. Zia Company, 5 FEP 1207 (1973).

Chrisner v. Compete Auto Transit, Inc., 25 FEP Cases 484 (1981).

Connecticut v. Teal, 29 FEP 1 (1982).

EEOC Decision No. 72-07034, FEP 435 (1971).

EEOC v. Detroit Edison, 10 FEP 239 (1975).

EEOC v. Sandia Corporation, 23 FEP 810 (1980).

EEOC v. Sears, Roebuck and Company, 39 FEP 1672 (1986).

Firefighters Institute v. City of St. Louis, 14 FEP 1486 (1977).

Friend v. Leidinger, 446 F. Supp. 361 (E.D. Va. 1977), *aff'd.,* 588 F.2d 61 (4th Cir. 1978).

Golden Rule Insurance Company et al. v. Washburn, et al., No. 419-76 (1984).

Great Lakes Chemical Corporation, Labor Relations Reference Manual 134 (May 22, 1990), 1276

Griggs v. Duke Power Company, 3 FEP 175 (1971).

Hester v. Southern Railway Company, 8 FEP 646 (1974).

Johnson v. Goodyear Tire and Rubber Company, 7 FEP 627 (1974).

King v. New Hampshire Department of Human Resources and Economic Development, 15 FEP 669 (1977).

Larry, P. v. Riles, 495 F. Supp. 926 (N.D. Cal.) (1979).

McDonald v. Santa Fe Trail Transportation Company, 427 U.S. 273 (1976).

Nash v. Jacksonville, BNA Employee Relations Weekly (August 13, 1990).

Pegues v. Mississippi State Employment Service, 22 FEP 392 (1980).

Pettway v. American Cast Iron Pipe Company, 7 FEP 1115 (1974).

Presbyterian Hospital, Labor Relations Reference Manual, 131, 180 (July 31, 1989).

Regents of the University of California v. Bakke, 438 U.S. 265 (1978).

Reynolds v. Sheet Metal Workers, 25 FEP 837 (1981).

Rogers v. International Paper Company, 10 FEP 404 (1975).

Rowe v. General Motors, 4 FEP 445 (1972).

Soroka v. Dayton Hudson Corporation, Cal CtApp No. A052157 (1991).

Spurlock v. United Airlines, 5 FEP Cases 17 (1972).

Statsny v. Southern Bell Telephone and Telegraph Company, 23 FEP 631 (1978).

United States v. Hazelwood School District, 11 EPD 10854 (1976).

United States v. Georgia Power Company, 5 FEP 587 (1973).

Wade v. Mississippi Cooperative Extention Service, 372 F. Supp. 126, 7 FEP 282 (1974).

Watkins v. Scott Paper Company, 12 FEP 1191 (1976).

Watson v. Fort Worth Bank and Trust Company, S. Ct., 86-6139 (June 29, 1988).

Weiner v. County of Oakland, 14 FEP 380 (1976).

Abbreviations:

Fair Employment Practice Cases (FEP)
Employment Practices Decisions (EPD)

REFERENCES

Adler, T. (1992, October). Personality, like plaster, is pretty stable over time. *APA Monitor*, p. 18.

Adler, T. (1993, January). Separate gender norms on tests raise questions. *APA Monitor*, p. 6.

Allen, W. B. (1988). Rhodes handicapping, or slowing the pace of integration. *Journal of Vocational Behavior, 33*, 365-378.

American Psychological Association (1974). *Standards for educational and psychological tests*, Washington, DC.

American Psychological Association (1985). *Standards for educational and psychological tests*, Washington, DC.

Anastasi, A. (1976). *Psychological testing* (4th ed.). New York: Macmillan.

Arnold, D. (1992, August). Integrity testing—good or bad? *Personnel Journal*.

Arvey, R. (1972). Some comments on culture fair tests. *Personnel Psychology, 25*, 433-448.

Arvey, R. (1979). *Fairness in selecting employees*, Menlo Park, CA: Addison-Wesley.

Arvey, R., & Faley, R. (1988). *Fairness in selecting employees*, (2nd ed.), Menlo Park, CA: Addison-Wesley.

Arvey, R., & McGowen, S. (1983). The use of experience requirements in selecting employees: A legal review. *Personnel Selection and Training Bulletin, 4*, 28-41.

Arvey, R., Miller, H., Gould, R., & Birch, P. (1987). Interview validity for selecting sales clerks. *Personnel Psychology, 40*, 1-12.

Avolio, B. J. (1982). Age stereotypes in interview evaluation contexts. *Dissertation Abstracts International, 42*, 3020B. (University Microfilms No. 81-29, 504).

Barrett, G. V., & Depinet, R. L. (1991). A reconsideration of testing for competence rather than intelligence. *American Psychologist, 46*, 1012-1024.

Bass, B. M., & Barrett, G. V. (1981). *People, work and organizations*. Boston: Allyn and Bacon.

Bentz, V. J. (1968). The Sears experience in the investigation, description, and prediction of executive behavior. In J. A. Myers, Jr. (Ed.), *Predicting managerial success*. Ann Arbor: Foundation for Research on Human Behavior.

Bentz, V. J. (1985). *A view from the top: A 30-year perspective of research devoted to the discovery, description, and prediction of executive behavior*. Paper presented to the American Psychological Association, Los Angeles.

Bolick, C. (1988). Legal policy aspects of testing. *Journal of Vocational Behavior, 33*, 320-330.

Borman, W. (1991). Job behavior, performance, and effectiveness. In M. D. Dunnette & L. M. Hough (Eds.), *Handbook of Industrial and Organizational Psychology: Vol. II*. Palo Alto, CA: Consulting Psychologists Press, Inc.

Bray, D., Campbell, R., & Grant, D. (1974). *Formative years in business: a long term AT&T study of manager alives*. New York: Wiley.

Brehm, S., & Kassen, S. (1990). *Social psychology*. Boston: Houghton, Mifflin.

Brown, S. H. (1978). Long-term validity of a personal history item scoring procedure. *Journal of Applied Psychology, 63,* 673-676.

Campbell, J. (1991). Modeling the performance prediction problem. In M. D. Dunnette & L. M. Hough (Eds.). *Handbook of Industrial and Organizational Psychology, Vol. I.* Palo Alto, CA: Consulting Psychologists Press, Inc.

Campbell, J., Pike, L., Flaugher, R., & Mahoney, M. (1970, October). *The prediction of supervisor's ratings from aptitude tests using a cross-ethnic cross-validation procedure.* (PR-70-18) Educational testing service.

Canter, F. (1963). Simulation on the California Psychological Inventory and the adjustment of the simulator. *Journal of Consulting Psychology, 27,* 253-256.

Carter, R., & Swanson, J. (1990). The validity of the Strong Interest Inventory with black americans: A review of the literature. *Journal of Vocational Behavior, 36,* 195-209.

Carton, B. (1989, February 19). *Drugs, silent killer of profits.* Boston Globe, p. A1.

Cattell, R. B., Eber, H. W., & Tatsuoka, M. M. (1970). *Handbook for the sixteen personality factor questionnaire,* Champaign, IL: IPAT.

Cecil, E., Paul, R., & Olins, R. (1973). Perceived importance of selected variables used to evaluate male and female job applicants. *Personnel Psychology, 76,* 397-404.

Childs, A., & Klimoski, R. J. (1986). Successfully predicting career success: An application of the biographical inventory. *Journal of Applied Psychology, 71,* 3-8.

Chin, C., Donn., J., & Conry, R. (1991). Effects of computer-based tests on the achievement, anxiety, and attitudes of grade 10 science students. *Educational and Psychological Measurement, 51,* 735-745.

Costa, P., & McCrae, R. (1984). Personality as a determinant of life-long well-being. In C. Malatest and C. Izard (Eds.). *Affective processes in adult development and aging.* Beverly Hills: Sage.

Costa, P., & McCrae, R. (1985). *The NEO personality inventory manual.* Odessa, FL: Psychological Assessment Resources.

Costa, P., McCrae, к., & Holland, J. (1984). Personality and vocational interests in an adult sample. *Journal of Applied Psychology, 69,* 390-400.

Cronbach, L. (1960). *Essentials of psychological testing.* New York: Harper and Rowe.

Davis, C., & Cowles, M. (1989). Automated psychological testing: Method of administration, need for approval and measures of anxiety. *Educational and Psychological Measurement, 49,* 311-320.

Day, D. V., & Silverman, S. B. (1989). Personality and job performance: Evidence of incremental validity. *Personnel Psychology, 42,* 25-36.

Dipboye, R. L., & Wiley, J. W. (1975, May/June). *Women as managers and stereotypes and realities.* Survey of Business, Center for Business and Economic Research, The University of Tennessee, *10,* 22-25.

Dipboye, R., & Phillips, A. (1989). Correlational tests of predictions from a process model of the interview. *Journal of Applied Psychology, 74,* 41-52.

DePaulo, B., & Pfeifer, R. (1986). On-the-job experience and skill at detecting deception. *Journal of Applied Social Psychology, 16,* 249-267.

DePaulo, B., Stone, J., & Lassiter, G. (1985). Deceiving and detecting deceit. In B. R. Schlenker (Ed.), *The self and social life.* New York: McGraw Hill.

Drakeley, R. J., Herriot, P., & Jones, A. (1988). Biographical data, training success and turnover. *Journal of Occupational Psychology, 61*, 145-152.

Drasgow, F. (1987). Study of measurement bias in two standardized tests. *Journal of Applied Psychology, 72*, 19-29

Drasgow, F., & Hulin, C. L. (1991). Item response theory. In M. D. Dunnette & L. M. Hough (Eds.), *Handbook of Industrial and Organizational Psychology: Vol. I* (pp. 577-636). Palo Alto, CA: Consulting Psychologists Press, Inc.

Drexler, M. (1990, May 27). *Employee drug-testing enters mainstream*. Des Moines Register, IC.

Dunnette, M. (1966). *Personnel selection and placement*. Belmont: Wadsworth Publishing Company.

Dunnette, M., & Borman, W. (1979). Personnel selection and classifications systems. *Annual Review of Psychology, 30*, 477-525.

Dunnette, M. D., Kirchner, W. K., Erickson, J., & Banas, P. (1960). Predicting turnover among female office workers. *Personnel Administration, 23*, 45-50.

Edwards, D. S., Hahn, C. P., & Fleishman, E. A. (1977). Evaluation of laboratory methods for the study of driver behavior: Relations between simulator and street performance. *Journal of Applied Psychology, 62*, 559-566.

Ekman, P., & O'Sullivan, M. (1991). Who can catch a liar? *American Psychologist, 46*, 913-920.

Equal Employment Opportunity Commission (1978, August 25). Civil Service Commission, Dept. of Labor and Dept. of Justice. Uniform guidelines on employee selection procedures, *Federal Register, 43* (No. 166) 38290-38315.

Ernst and Young. (1992, January). *International mass retail association survey of retail loss prevention trends*. Chain Store Age Executive.

Evan, W., & Miller, J. (1969). Differential effects on response bias of computer v. conventional administration of a social science questionnaire. *Behavioral Science, 14*, 216-227.

Fearnside, W., & Holther, W. (1959). *Fallacy the counterfeit of argument*, Englewood Cliffs: Prentice Hall.

Finlayson, D. (1991, July 23). *Hiring and Firing*. Texas Society of Certified Public Accountants Conference, Infomart, Dallas.

Fisher, R., & Ury, W. (1981). *Getting to yes*. New York: Penguin.

Freiberg, P., & DeAngelis, T. (1992). High court to review on hiring tests. *APA Monitor, 23*.

Gazner, B. (1990, May 27). Should you tell all? *Parade*.

Genua, R. L. (1979). *The employer's guide to interviewing*. Englewood Cliffs, NJ: Prentice-Hall.

Ghiselli, E. E. (1966). The validity of a personnel interview. *Personnel Psychology, 19*, 389-394

Ghiselli, E. E. (1973). The validity of aptitude tests in personnel selection. *Personnel Psychology, 26*, 461-477.

Goldberg, L. R. (1993). The structure of phenotypic personality traits. *American Psychologist, 48*, 26-34.

Goldstein, B., & Patterson, P. (1988). Turning back the Title VII clock: the resegregation of the American Work Force through validity generalization. *Journal of Vocational Behavior, 33*,452-462.

Goldstein, I. (1991). Training in work organizations. In M. D. Dunnette & L. M. Hough (Eds.), *Handbook of Industrial and Organizational Psychology* (pp. 507-620). Palo Alto, CA: Consulting Psychologists Press, Inc.

Gollub, L., & Campion, J. (1991, April). *The Employment Interview on Trial.* Paper presented to SIOP, University of Houston, TX .

Gordon, R. A., Lewis, M. A., & Quigley, A. M. (1988). Can we count on muddling through the *g* crisis in employment? *Journal of Vocational Behavior, 33*, 424-451.

Gordon, R. A., Rozelle, R. M., & Baxter, J. C. (1988). The effect of applicant age, job level, and accountability of the evaluation of job applicants. *Organization Behavior Human Decision Process, 41*, 20-33.

Gormly, J. (1985). Review of Guilford Zimmerman temperament survey, *Buros 9th Mental Measurement Year Book.*

Gottfredson, L. S. (1988). Reconsidering fairness: A matter of social and ethical priorities. *Journal of Vocational Behavior, 33*, 293-319.

Graham, J. R. (1987). *The MMPI: a practical guide.* New York: Oxford University Press.

Greve, M. (1992, October 5). The newest move in law school's quota game. *Wall Street Journal*, A12.

Guilford, J. (1950). *Fundamentals statistics in psychology and education.* New York: McGraw Hill.

Guilford, J., Zimmerman, W., & Guilford, J. (1976). *The Guilford Zimmerman temperament survey handbook.* San Diego: EDITS.

Guion, R. (1991). Personnel assessment, selection and placement. In M. D. Dunnette & L. M. Hough (Eds.), *Handbook of Industrial and Organizational Psychology, Vol. II* (pp. 327-398). Palo Alto, CA: Consulting Psychologists Press.

Guion, R., & Gottier, R. (1965). Validity of personality measures in personnel selection. *Personnel Psychology, 18*, 135-164.

Gutenberg, R., Arvey, R., Osburn, H., & Jeanneret, P. (1983). Moderating effects of decision-making/information processing job dimensions on test validities. *Journal of Applied Psychology, 68*, 602-608.

Haefner, J. E.(1977). Race, age, sex and competence as factors in employee selection of the disadvantaged. *Journal of Applied Psychology, 62*, 199-202.

Hansen, J. C., & Campbell, D. P. (1985). *Manual for the SVIB-SCII.* Palo Alto, CA: Consulting Psychologists Press.

Harrell, T. (1969). The personality of high earning MBA's in big business. *Personnel Psychology, 22*, 457-463.

Harrell, T. (1970). The personality of high earning MBA's in small business. *Personnel Psychology, 23*, 369-375.

Harrell, T. (1972). High earning MBA's. *Personnel Psychology, 25*, 523-530.

Harrell, T., & Harrell, M. (1973). The personality of MBA's who reach general management early. *Personnel Psychology, 26*, 127-134.

Harrell, T., & Harrell, M. (1984). *Stanford MBA careers: A 20-year longitudinal study* (Research paper No. 723). Stanford, CA: Stanford University.

Hayes, W. L. (1973). *Statistics for the Social Sciences.* New York: Holt, Rinehart, & Winston.

Heilman, M., Martell, R., & Simon, M. (1988). The vagaries of sex bias: conditions regulating the undervaluation, equivaluation, and overvaluation of female job applications. *Organ. Behav. Hum Decis. Process.*, *41*, 98-110.

Helmreick, R., Sawin, L., & Carsrud, A. (1986). The honeymoon effect in job performance. *Journal of Applied Psychology*, *71*, 185-188.

Helms, J. E. (1992). Why is there no study of cultural equivalence in standardized cognitive ability testing? *American Psychologist*, *47*, 1083-1101.

Hersey, P., & Blanchard, K. (1982). *Management of Organizational Behavior.* Englewood Cliffs, NJ: Prentice-Hall.

Higgins, C., & Silvers, C. (1958). A comparison Stanford-Binet and colored raven progressive matrices IQ for children with low socioeconomic status. *Journal of Consulting Psychology*, *22*, 565-568.

Hogan, R.T. (1991). Personality and Personality measurement. *Handbook of Industrial and Organizational Psychology, (Vol. II).* Palo Alto, CA: Consulting Psychologists Press, Inc.

Holland, J. (1979). *The Self-directed search manual.* Palo Alto, CA: Consulting Psychologists Press.

Holland, J. (1985). Vocational preference inventory manual. Odessa, FL: Psychological Assessment Resources.

Holland, J. (1992). Making vocational choices. Odessa, FL: Psychological Assessment Resources.

Hollenbeck, J., & Whitener, E. (1988). Criterion-related validation for small sample contexts: an integrated approach to synthetic validity. *Journal of Applied Psychology*, *73*, 536-544.

Howard, A., & Bray, D. W. (1988). *Managerial lives in transition.* New York: Guilford.

Hughes, J. F., Dunn, J. F., & Baxter, B. (1956). The validity of selection instruments under operating conditions. *Personnel Psychology*, *9*, 321-324.

Human Resource Executive (1992, May). *Survey on testing,* 46-47.

Hunter, J., & Hunter, F. (1984). Validity and utility of alternate predictors of performance. *Psychological Bulletin*, *96*, 72-98.

Inwald, R. E. (1988). Five-year follow-up study of departmental terminations as predicted by 16 preemployment psychological indicators. *Journal of Applied Psychology*, *73*, 703-710.

Jackson, S. E., & Schuler, R. S. (1990). Human resource planning. *American Psychologist*, *45*, 223-239.

Janz, T. (1982). Initial comparisons of pattern behavior description interviews vs. unstructured interviews. *Journal of Applied Psychology*, *67*, 577-580.

Johnson, A. & Cottle, W. C. (1952). The Guilford-Zimmerman Temperament Survey: III With negro urban high school students. *University of Kansas Bulletin of Education*, *6*, 75-80.

Jones, L., & Appelbaum, M. (1989). Psychometric methods. *Annual Review Psychology*, *40*, 23-43.

Judson, H. F. (1987). *The Search for solutions.* Baltimore, MD: Johns Hopkins University Press.

Karlins, M., Coffman, T., & Walters, G. (1969). On the fading of social stereotypes: Studies in three generations of college students. *Journal of Personality and Social Psychology, 13*, 1-16.

King, M., Jr. (1992). *I have a dream.* James Washington, (Ed.) San Francisco: Harper.

Kleiman, L., & Faley, R. (1985). The implications of professional and legal guidelines for court decisions involving criterion-related validity: A review and analysis. *Personnel Psychology, 38*, 803-833.

Kohnken, G. (1987). Training police officers to detect deceptive eye-witness statements: Does it work? *Social Behavior, 2*, 1-17.

Korn, L. (1988). *The success profile.* New York: Simon and Schuster.

Kotter, J. P. (1982, November-December). What effective general managers really do. *Harvard Business Review*, 156-167.

Kraut, R. (1980). Humans as lie detectors: Some second thoughts. *Journal of Communication, 30*, 209-216.

Kraut, R., & Poe, D. (1980). On the line: The deception judgments of customs inspectors and layman. *Journal of Personality and Social Psychology, 39*, 784-798.

Kunde, D. (1992, March 31). Big Business. *Dallas Morning News*, IA.

Latham, G. P., & Saari, L. M. (1984). Do people do what they say? Further studies on the situational interview. *Journal of Applied Psychology, 69*, 569-573.

Latham, G. P., Saari, L. M., Pursell, E. D., & Campion, M. A. (1980). The situational interview. *Journal of Applied Psychology, 65*, 422-427.

Levin, H. M. (1988). Issues of agreement and contention in employment testing. *Journal of Vocational Behavior, 33*, 398-403.

Lifson, K. A. (1976). *Winners—how to hire them and keep them in your organization.* Young Presidents Organization University, Vienna.

Lord, F. (1962). Cutting scores and errors of measurement. *Psychometrika, 27*, 19-30.

Lord, F. (1963). Cutting scores and errors of measurement: A second case. *Educational and Psychological Measurement, 23*, 63-68.

Lublin, J. S. (1991, December 31). Rights law to spur shifts in promotions. *Wall Street Journal*, B1.

Lukin, M., Dowd, E., Plake, B., & Kraft, R. (1985). Comparing computerized vs. traditional psychological assessment. *Computers in Human Behavior, 1*, 49-58.

Lykken, D., & Rose, R. (1963). Psychological prediction from actuarial tables. *Journal of Clinical Psychology, 19*, 139-151.

McClelland, D. C. (1973). Testing for competence rather than for "intelligence." *American Psychologist, 28*, 1-14.

McCormick, E. J., & Ilgen, D. (1980). *Industrial psychology.* Englewood Cliffs, NJ: Prentice-Hall.

McCoy, A. (1989, February 19). *Thieves among us.* Pittsburgh Press.

McDaniel, M., & Schmidt, F. L. (1985, April). *A meta-analysis of the validity of training and experience ratings in personnel selection* (Report No. OSP-85-1). U.S. Office of Personnel Management.

McDaniel, M. A., Whetzel, D. L., Schmidt, F. L., Maurer, S., & Russel, J. (1988). *The validity of employment interviews: A review and meta-analysis.* (unpublished paper, cited in Schmidt).

McKenna, D. D., & Wright, P. M. (1992). Alternative metaphors for organization design. In M. D. Dunnette & L. M. Hough (Eds.), *Handbook of Industrial and Organizational Psychology: Vol. III.* (pp. 327-398). Palo Alto, CA: Consulting Psychologists Press, Inc.

McMurry, R. N. (1947). Validating the patterned interview. *Personnel, 23,* 263-272.

Meehl, P. E. (1957). When shall we use our heads instead of the formula? *Journal of Counseling Psychology, 4,* 268-273.

Meyer, H. (1987). Predicting supervisory ratings versus promotional progress in test validation studies. *Journal of Applied Psychology, 72,* 696-697.

Miner, M., & Miner, J. (1978). *Employee selection within the law.* Bureau of National Affairs, Washington, DC.

Mitchell, E. (1992, January 15) *To test or not to test, legal considerations in employment testing.* Memorandum. Thompson, Hine and Flory Attorneys at Law, Cincinnati, OH.

Moore, C., MacNaughton, J., and Osburn, H. (1969). Ethnic differences within an industrial selection battery. *Personnel Psychology, 22,* 473-482.

Mossholder, K. , & Arvey, R. (1984). Synthetic validity: a conceptual and comparative review. *Journal of Applied Psychology, 69,* 322-333.

Mumford, M.D., & Owens, W. A. (1987). Methodology review: principles, procedures, and findings in the application of background data measures. *Applied Psychology Measurement, 11,* 1-31.

Norton, E. H. (1977). *Minutes of commission meeting of December 22.* U.S. Equal Employment Opportunity Commission (As quoted in Sharf, 1988).

Olsen, J., Maynes, D., Slawson, D., & Ho, K. (1989). Comparisons of paper-administered, computer-administered and computerized adaptive achievement test. *Journal of Ed. Computing Research, 5.*

Orpen, C. (1985). Patterned behavior description interviews vs. unstructured interviews. *Journal of Applied Psychology, 70,* 774-776.

Pace, L. A., & Schoenfeldt, L. F. (1977). Legal concerns in the use of weighted application blanks. *Personnel Psychology, 30,* 159-166.

Peters, T., & Waterman, R. (1982). *Search for excellence.* New York: Harper and Row.

Pulley, B. (1992, December 21). Strained family. *The Wall Street Journal,* A1.

Raza, S. M., & Carpenter, B. N. (1987). A model of hiring decisions in real employment interviews. *Journal of Applied Psychology, 72,* 596-603.

Rose, R. G. (1980, March 24). Tests not only device frowned on by EEOC. *Dallas/Fort Worth Business.*

Rose, R. G. (1984). The use of conditional probabilities in applications of Holland's theory. *Journal of Vocational Behavior, 25,* 284-289.

Rose, R. G. (1992, December). Men and women in management. *Dallas Psychologist,* 7-8.

Rose, R. G., & Holland, J. L. (1985). *Vocational Preference Inventory: Computer Version.* Odessa, FL: Psychological Assessment Resources, Inc.

Rothstein, H. R., Schmidt, F. L., Erwin, F. W., Owens, W. A., & Sparks, C. P. (1990). Biographical data in employment selection: Can validities be made generalizable? *Journal of Applied Psychology, 75,* 175-184.

Ruch, G., & Ruch, W. (1963). *EAS Technical Report.* Los Angeles: Psychological Services.

Ryan, A., & Lasek, M. (1991). Negligent hiring and defamation: Areas of liability related to pre-employment inquiries. *Personnel Psychology, 44.*

Sackett, P., Burris, L., & Callahan, C. (1989). Integrity testing for personnel selection: An update. *Personnel Psychology, 42,* 491-529.

Sackett, P., & Harris, M. (1984). Honesty testing for personnel selection: A review and critique. *Personnel Psychology, 37,* 221-225.

Schein, E. H. (1980). *Organizational psychology.* Englewood Cliffs, NJ: Prentice-Hall.

Schein, V. (1973). The relationship between sex role stereotypes and requisite management characteristics. *Journal of Applied Psychology, 57,* 95-100.

Schmidt, F. (1988). The problem of group differences in ability test scores in employment selection. *Journal of Vocational Behavior, 33,* 272-292.

Schmidt, F., & Hunter, J. (1981). Employment testing: Old theories and new research findings. *American Psychologist, 36,* 1128-1137.

Schmidt, F., Hunter, J., Croll, P., & McKenzie, R. (1983). Estimation of employment test validities by expert judgment. *Journal of Applied Psychology, 68,* 590-601.

Schmidt, F., Hunter, J., Outerbridge, A., & Goff, S. (1988). Joint relation of experience and ability with job performance: Test of three hypotheses. *Journal of Applied Psychology, 73,* 46-47.

Schmidt, F., Hunter, J., Pearlman, K., & Hirsh, H. (1985). Forty questions about validity generalization and meta-analysis. *Personnel Psychology, 38,* 697-798.

Schmidt, F., Ones, D., & Hunter, J. (1992). Personnel selection. *Annual Review of Psychology, 43,* 627-670.

Schmitt, N., & Robertson, I. (1990). Personnel selection. *Annual Review of Psychology, 41,* 289-319.

Schmitt, N., Gooding, R., Noe, R., & Kirsch, M. (1984). Meta-analysis of validity studies published between 1964 and 1982 and the investigation of study characteristics. *Personnel Psychology, 37,* 407-422.

Schroeder, D., & Costa, P. (1984). Influence of life events stress on physical illness: Substantive effects or methodological flaws. *Journal of Personality and Social Psychology, 46,* 853-863.

Seymour, R. (1988). Why plaintiff's counsel challenge tests, and how can successfully challenge the theory of "validity generalization." *Journal of Vocational Behavior, 33,* 331-364.

Sharf, J. (1988). Litigating personnel measurement policy. *Journal of Vocational Behavior, 33,* 235-271.

Shuh, A. L. (1967). The predictability of employment tenure: A review of the literature. *Personnel Psychology, 20,* 133-152.

Society for Industrial-Organizational Psychology (1987). *Principles for the validitation and use of personnel selection procedures.* College Park, MD: American Psychological Association.

Sorenson, L. L. (1966, May). *Test Data Report* (Report #51). New York: Harcourt Brace and World.

Sorenson, W. W. (1964). *Configural scoring of biographical items for predicting sales success.* Unpublished Ph.D. Dissertation. Minneapolis, MN: University of Minnesota.

Sparks, C. P. (1983). Paper and pencil measures of potential. In G. F. Dreher & P. R. Sackett (Eds.). *Perspectives on employee staffing and selection* (pp. 349-368). Homewood, IL: Irwin.

Spearman, C. (1927). *The abilities of man.* London: MacMillan.

Stogdill, R. (1974). *Handbook of leadership: A survey of theory and research.* New York: Free Press.

Tenopyr, M. (1967). *Race and socio-economic status as moderators predicting machine-shop training success.* Paper presented at symposium at American Psychological Association Convention, Washington, DC.

Tenopyr, M., & Oeltjen, P. (1982). Personnel selection and classification. *Annual Review of Psychology, 33,* 581-618.

Thayer, P. W. (1977). Something old, something new. *Personnel Psychology, 30,* 513-524.

Thernstrom, A. (1992, November 18). Affirmative action backfires at Harvard Law Review. *Wall Street Journal.*

Thorndike, R. L. (1986). The role of general ability in prediction. *Journal of Vocational Behavior, 29,* 332-339.

Thornton, G. C.,III, & Byham, W. C. (1982). *Assessment centers and managerial performance.* San Diego: Academic Press.

Turkington, C. (1992, December). Ruling opens door—a crack—to IQ-testing some black kids. *APA Monitor.*

U.S. Congress, Office of Technology Assessment (1990, September). *The use of integrity tests for pre-employment screening* (Publication No. ota-set-442). Washington, DC: U.S. Government Printing Office.

Watson, G., & Glaser, E. (1980). *Watson-Glaser critical thinking appraisal manual.* New York: The Psychological Corporation.

Webster, E. C. (1964). *Decision making in the employment interview.* Montreal: Industrial Relations Center, McGill University.

Wechsler, D. (1981). *WAIS-R manual.* New York: Psychological Corporation.

Weiner, Y., & Vaitenas, R. (1977). Personality correlates for voluntary midcareer change in enterprising occupations. *Journal of Applied Psychology, 62,* 706-712.

Wernimont, P. F. (1962). Reevaluation of a weighted application blank for office personnel. *Journal of Applied Psychology, 46,* 417-419.

Wigdor, A. K., & Garner, W. R. (1982). *Ability testing: Uses, consequences, and controversies: Part I.* Report of the Committee, Washington, DC: National Academy Press.

Williams, R. L. (1975). *Black intelligence test of cultural homogeneity: Manual of directions.* St. Louis, MO: Williams and Associates, Inc.

Willingham, W. W. (1974). Predicting success in graduate education. *Science, 183,* 273-278.

Wise, S., & Plake, B. (1989). Research on the effects of administering tests via computers. *Educational Measurement Issues and Practice, 8,* 5-10.

Wonderlic E. F. (1992). *Wonderlic personnel test and scholastic level exam user's manual.* Libertyville, IL: Wonderlic Personnel Test, Inc.

Yukl, G. A. (1981). *Leadership in organizations.* Englewood Cliffs, NJ: Prentice-Hall.

Yukl, G. A., & Van Fleet, D. D. (1992). Theory and research on leadership. *Handbook of Industrial and Organizational Psychology: Vol. III* (pp. 147-198). Palo Alto, CA: Consulting Psychologists Press, Inc.

Zaccarro, S. J., Foti, R. J., & Kenney, D. A. (1992). Self-monitoring and trait-based variance in leadership: An investigation of leader flexibility across multiple group situations. *Journal of Applied Psychology, 76*, 179-185.

Zedeck, S., & Cascio, W. (1984). Psychological issues in personnel decisions. *Annual Review of Psychology, 35*, 461-518.

Zuckerman, M., DePaulo, B., & Rosenthal, R. (1981). Verbal and nonverbal communication of deception. In L. Berkowitz (Ed.). *Advances in experimental social psychology, Vol. 14*. San Diego: Academic Press.

GLOSSARY

Statistical Concepts

Alternate form. Another version of a test that is similar enough to be used interchangeably.

Correction for guessing. Formulae used to cancel out the effect of guessing.

Correlation. A correlation is a statistical formula that expresses how strongly one measurement is related to another, varying from 0 to 1, with a negative prefix if the relationship is inverse, that is, one measure increases as the other decreases.

Cut score. The minimum score necessary for passing.

Descriptive statistics. A descriptive statistic is one that describes some aspect of a group of scores (e.g., the average) versus an inferential statistic (one that is used to establish statistical significance).

Expectancy table. A table of scores showed the probability of success associated with each level of test score.

Hits and false positives. A *hit* is the probability of categorizing something as x, given that it is x. A *false positive* is the probability of categorizing something as x, given that it is not x. A *miss* is 1 – *hit*; a *correct rejection* is 1 – *false positive*.

Ipsatative. When a person's score refers to a relative ranking of the person's own interests or traits as opposed to a normative comparison to other people. For example, you might know that Jim is more introverted than extraverted, but you might not know how introverted compared to other people.

Inferential statistic. A family of statistics used to establish whether two measures are related in a significant manner, that is, there is a relationship that is not merely due to chance.

Mean. The arithmetic average of a distribution of scores. In a normal distribution, equal to the mode and the median.

Median. The score that is at the 50th percentile, right in the middle of a distribution. In a normal distribution, equal to the mode and the mean.

Meta-analysis. A research procedure that involves correction of statistical results in order to pool results from various studies.

Mode. The most frequent score in a distribution. In a normal distribution, equal to the mode and the mean.

Moderator Variable. Sometimes a test or other predictor will be more precise for various subgroups. If you found that a test was a stronger predictor for young people than older people, age would be said to be a *moderator variable* for your test.

Multiple R. Like a correlation, but with more than one predictive measure.

Norm group. The type of group used as a standard for interpreting scores.

Normally distributed. A distribution of scores refers to the frequency, or how often, each score occurs. A normal distribution has mostly moderate scores with about as many high as there are low. It looks like a bell when graphed.

Percentile. The percentage of people at or below a score is the score's percentile.

Population. The entirety of a group.

Race norming. Using different percentile conversions for different races or groups.

Ratings. Rating scales are often used in measuring human behavior.

Raw score. The score before being transformed, for example, given in percentile form.

Restriction of range. A distribution of scores that is limited, making statistical inferences difficult. If everyone in the class makes 99 or 100, there's not enough range to determine any relationship, even if it exists.

Sample. A subset of a large population used to make inferences about the population.

Statistically significant. A statistic result is significant if it is unlikely to be due to chance (the probability is 5/100 or lower).

Test battery. A group of tests that are administered together.

Utility. Utility refers to the practical effect on business.

Validity correlation. The correlation between the test and the criterion is a measure of criterion validity. The higher the correlation, the more valid the test.

Weight. One test may be more important than another. Statistically, this is captured by different weights for different factors. I may add test 1 score twice and test 2 score only once; test 1 is *weighted* more heavily.

Legal Terminology

ADA. Americans With Disabilities Act. This act has implications for the use of medical examination in hiring but also has implications for the types of items that can be asked on application blanks. As of 1992, it is relatively new and untested, but it should be monitored because it could have impact on psychological testing, depending on the manner in which "disability" and "medical" are interpreted in case law.

Adverse Impact. Hiring members of a group at a disproportionately low rate.

Affirmative Action. A method of preferential hiring for a certain group to remedy imbalance due to past unjust hiring practices.

EEOC. Equal Employment Opportunity Commission, the agency that enforces Title VII and other relevant employment laws.

EEOC Uniform Guidelines. Equal Employment Opportunity Commission Uniform Guidelines (1978)(UG). These are guidelines for determining when validation is necessary (it is not in all cases) and also sets standards for test validation in those cases where validation is necessary.

Negligent Hiring. Negligent hiring, *respondeat superior* and other concepts revolve around the idea that the employer is responsible for the actions of people hired. In some cases, employers can get in trouble for not learning enough about the people they hire.

Selection device. The Uniform Guidelines define a selection device as anything used in selection: written tests, interviews, experience requirements or anything else. (See Uniform Guidelines §16Q.)

Testing Terminology

Ability or aptitude tests. Tests of cognitive or motor abilities. Ability refers to a present skill and aptitude to the ability to gain such ability; in practice there may be very little distinction.

Biodata and Weighted Application Blanks. Biodata refers to information about an individual's past (e.g., education, experience, number of siblings) information that is often contained on an application blank. Biodata can be coded as variables and weighted in a multiple regression equation or some other mathematical formula. It can then be scored as a test.

Cognitive test. A commonly used term for intellectual ability and achievement tests. Schmidt (1988, p. 272) gives, as examples of cognitive abilities, those tests of "verbal, quantitative, spatial or mechanical abilities." A basic *g* factor (for general intelligence) is thought to underlie cognitive tests.

Interest inventory. These instruments ask about job and work interest preferences. In practice, these are often close to personality inventories, for example, people who express a preference for sales activities are often more outgoing than those who express a preference for mechanical tasks.

Selection Ratio. The proportion of people applying for a job that will actually be hired. If the ratio is low, it means you can afford to be choosey and may fail to hire people that were really qualified. If the ratio is high, it means you will probably hire some people who are not qualified.

Personality inventory. Often referred to as personality tests or psychological tests, these tests measure personality traits such as sociability or neuroticism.

Specific achievement tests. Tests of specific knowledge such as testing someone's knowledge of General Motors truck engine repair.

Reliability and Validity

Criterion. The measure of success that a test measures.

Reliability. The extent to which a test reliably measures the same thing across time.

Validity. Refers to evidence that a test measures that which the user claims it measures.

- content validity—validity based on test content.
- criterion validity—validity based on prediction of a criterion.
- construct validity—validity based on theory.
- differential validity—validity that is different for the same selection device depending on the group (e.g., more valid for black than white, male than female).

- validity generalization—generalizing validity of a test across different but similar jobs.
- synthetic validity—building validity by looking at job components.

Psychological Concepts

Cognition. That aspect of the mind that involves planning, remembering, learning or using math and vocabulary. It may be useful in some cases to contrast general intelligence (e.g., ability to learn quickly, plan well) from specific skills (e.g., knowledge of algebra) even though the concepts may overlap a great deal.

Affect. That aspect of the mind that involves emotions such as anger, hatred, sorrow, joy, and happiness.

Personality. Those aspects of the mind reflected in traits that everyone has (such as sociability) that vary in intensity from one person to the next (some people are more outgoing than others). Such things as work interests may be related to personality; for example, people who have a personality trait of being outgoing and sociable will be more interested in sales than a person who is not very outgoing and sociable.

Types of Professionals

Psychometrician. A term sometimes used for psychologists who specialize in test development or analysis.

Psychiatrist. A physician (usually an M.D.) who has completed a residency in treatment of people with medical disorders. Psychiatrists and psychologists are often confused because both work with people with problems, both study the mind, and they often work together.

Psychologist, Clinical. A person, usually a Ph.D., who counsels with people about personal problems, but does not dispense medication. The person you usually think of when you think of a psychologist.

Human Resources Director. In some cases this title is mis-applied to people who really function as personnel clerks. In many cases, however, the Human Resourses Director or Vice President of Human Resources holds an important position. He/she will often perform some selection procedures (e.g., interviewing and some testing) and often serves as the gatekeeper for outside testing experts.

Psychologist Industrial/Organizational. A psychologist who works with business. Because a major business need is hiring and development, two things that are benefitted by testing, I/O Psychologists often work with testing.